A LITTLE
F'D UP

WHY
FEMINISIM
IS NOT A
DIRTY
WORD

JULIE ZEILINGER

SEAL PRESS

A LITTLE F'D UP
Why Feminism is Not a Dirty Word

Copyright © 2012 by Julie Zeilinger

Published by
Seal Press
A Member of the Perseus Books Group
1700 Fourth Street
Berkeley, California

Library of Congress Cataloging-in-Publication Data

Zeilinger, Julie, 1993-
  A little f'd up : why feminism is not a dirty word / Julie Zeilinger.
    p. cm.
  Includes bibliographical references.
  ISBN 978-1-58005-371-6
  1. Feminism—United States. 2. Young women—United States—
Attitudes. I. Title.
  HQ1421.Z447 2012
  305.420973—dc23
                              2011047093

9 8 7 6 5 4 3 2 1

Cover design by Elke Barter
Interior design by Domini Dragoone
Printed in the United States of America
Distributed by Publishers Group West

For Cathy, Scott, and Brian Zeilinger,
the most incredible and supportive family
in the entire world.

CONTENTS

FOREWORD

I can tell a lot about a person based on what they do when I first tell them I'm a feminist.

Some people will give you a skeptical look and say something along the lines of, "But you don't *look* like a feminist." These are the folks you can maybe talk some sense to, if they're open to hearing why anti-feminist stereotypes are so old school and ridiculous. Then there are the people (mostly men) who will feign fear and say, "Oooh, are you going to hit me?" or some other such nonsense that suggests you're too angry for your own good. These are people to avoid at all costs. Then there are the keepers—the folks who say, "Tell me more," or, "What's that like?" Those are the people that make my day. My year!

But stereotypes are damaging all around—and making judgments about people's reaction to the word or idea of feminism can be a mistake, too. Sometimes people will surprise you.

A young Australian man I met while I was traveling responded to my telling him I was a feminist by actually *lifting my arm and looking underneath for armpit hair.* Not a good sign; I thought for sure he was an irredeemable asshole. But, after some time getting to know each other outside of bizarre first impressions, we ended up becoming great friends and still keep in touch almost ten years later. The truth is, for a lot of people—even good, smart, well-intentioned people—feminism *is* a dirty word. Or a funny word. Or a scary one.

This isn't just the case for younger people, either (despite the stereotypes that it's young women who don't call themselves feminists). People who are wary of "feminism" come in all ages. Often these folks don't really know what feminism is about. They've maybe heard the bra-burning myth or seen mainstream media portrayals of feminists and have been put off. Or they're nervous about seeming uninformed about gender issues so they become defensive. Sometimes people have really good reasons for reacting negatively to the label feminism. The movement's focus on white, cis, middle-class issues has left a lot of people, rightfully, skeptical or hurt. It's a reality we can't ignore.

Feminists and people who care about gender justice need to take a close look why feminism is still so disparaged, no matter what the reason. In large part, it's because there's been a well-organized social and political antifeminist movement dedicated to making sure that people, women especially, eschew the feminism and the ideas behind it. Whether it's conservative radio hosts calling feminists "feminazis" or right-wing women's organizations suggesting that equality actually *hurts* women, there's a reason that so many people think so little of a movement that has done so much good.

The newest form of feminist-bashing is a bit more insidious than just straight up calling us frigid manhaters. In the last couple of years, instead of completely dismissing feminism, antifeminist groups have started calling themselves the "real" feminists. Groups like the Independent Women's Forum—who try to ban "The Vagina Monologues" on college campuses and argue that pay inequity doesn't exist—have figured out that the feminist label has power, and they're trying to co-opt it.

This is why I'm so glad that Julie has written this book. In a time when the very definition of feminism is up for grabs, when people who are feminists won't identify as such and people who are most definitely *not* feminists are trying to steal the language of the movement, we need a voice that gets past the bullshit. A clear, strong, young voice that lets people know what feminism is actually about. We have a lot of those voices online, so it's great to start to see some in print as well!

At the end of the day, whatever someone's reason for giving feminism the side-eye, what gives me hope is the knowledge that there's space for conversation, for listening, and for making connections with other people that can lead to a better, more just world. No matter what someone's initial reaction is to "feminism," there's room for growth and action—what more could we want?

—JESSICA VALENTI

INTRODUCTION

So. I'm a teenager and I wrote a book. And not just any book. A book about feminism.

What kind of *obviously* pretentious and generally ridiculous teen does that?

Well, I'm actually pretty typical. I grew up in Pepper Pike, Ohio, (seriously) and went to a small school that worshiped football, but if we had actually won a game, I think I would've immediately begun to collect canned goods and survival gear in preparation for the clearly imminent rapture. I have a hilarious older brother, two loving and supportive parents, and a dog who thinks he's a cat. I also started the FBomb: a loud, proud, snarky blog for young feminists that is read by hundreds of thousands of people from all over the world.

So how could a (relatively) normal young girl from Ohio (who, as we all know, should really be obsessed with boys, clothes, and ABC Family original programming) be both a regular teen and a prominent teenage feminist?

It all started in the eighth grade. For decades, my middle school has upheld the tradition of requiring all eighth graders to write a speech on a topic of their choice and deliver it to the entire school.

Now, to a bunch of fourteen-year-olds who just want to look cute in their skin-tight Abercrombie jeans, and who are constantly worried there's food stuck in their blue-and-magenta braces, standing in front of every single one of their peers and speaking publicly for ten minutes is terrifying, to say the least.

In sixth and seventh grade, kids are already starting to worry about the chapel talk. They mention it in hushed tones, quickly spat out, before changing the subject so as to not linger on its imminent reality. The school's obviously satanic teachers refer to it as a "public-speaking opportunity." But to 99.9 percent of eighth graders, it's really more like an opportunity to confirm our worst suspicions: that everybody is judging us, and *only* us. Anyway, at that point in our young lives, we are all planning on becoming things like Rihanna's backup dancers or professional dirt bikers, so *obviously* public speaking is a completely superfluous skill.

I tried to think positively about my speech. Despite the feeling of imminent doom, I realized that as a fourteen-year-old, it is incredibly difficult to get anyone to listen to you talk about anything serious for more than thirty seconds. And here I was, being handed a full ten minutes. I may have been terrified, but dammit, I was going to *use* those precious minutes. I was going to enlighten my audience of tweens and move them to greater social action. Local news organizations were going to be called to the scene after my talk, which was going to incite my prepubescent peers to riot against the newly revealed injustices of the world. I was going to give the *best speech ever*—that is, if I did not spontaneously throw up midspeech, which was also a real possibility.

Around the same time, my mom handed me an article she

found in a copy of *Glamour* magazine while in the dentist's waiting room. (Yeah, she stole it. So sue her. You made her wait forty minutes to get her teeth cleaned. *Call it even.*) It was titled "A Generation of Women Wiped Out?"[1] The article was about women in South Asia, particularly in India, who were killing their own baby girls just because of their disappointing gender.

Needless to say, I was deeply disturbed—not only by the horrific facts I'd been presented with, but also by the fact that neither I, nor anybody I knew, had even been aware that thousands of baby girls die every year because of this. And so I decided to write my speech about female feticide and infanticide, and I started pouring over the research. As it often happens, my research led me to all kinds of related issues, and I soon realized there were many more atrocities being committed against women all over the world—and even in my own country. And I kept thinking, *This can't be happening. If this were happening, everybody would be talking about it. I would have heard of it before. Everybody would be horrified. It would be on the news.* But when I checked the news, I saw only that Paris Hilton had bought her forty-seventh Chihuahua and that another married politician was wrapped up in a sex scandal.

This only added fuel to my internal fire. People had to learn what was happening. And I was going to tell them. So I proudly gave my impassioned speech to my entire school . . . to glazed eyes. For months, I was remembered as "the girl who gave the speech about dead babies."

Not quite the reaction I'd been hoping for.

But it was worth it, because it was around this time that I realized I was a feminist.

It wasn't that becoming a feminist was a predestined mission embedded deep in my genetic coding. There wasn't a moment when a light bulb flashed over my head and a hallelujah chorus of angels descended from feminist heaven to gently wrap me in a wreath woven from PLANNED PARENTHOOD bumper stickers. I didn't transition from nonfeminist to überfeminist overnight. Rather, the term speech spurred my awareness of feminism as a movement, and helped me realize that feminism accurately described my beliefs.

I don't remember the first time I told somebody I was a feminist. I don't remember when I first internally referred to myself as a feminist. I just know that after my speech, I was one. And it seemed like I was the only one.

Thankfully, when I got to high school, my advisor (a recent Harvard grad whose office wall boasted FEMINISTS FOR CHOICE and REPUBLICANS FOR VOLDEMORT bumper stickers) introduced me to the writing of third-wave feminists like Jessica Valenti and Courtney Martin. She also sent me the link to Feministing, one of the most-visited feminist blogs out there in the big, wide interwebs. I was hooked from day one. Here were intelligent women writing about things that actually mattered. It was entertaining, and I was actually learning. What a concept!

The only problem with Feministing and the other feminist blogs I began to read regularly was that, despite the overwhelming awesomeness of intelligent and relatively young female voices, teens and teen issues were virtually absent from the discussions. Yes, conversations about, say, work–life balance and whether or not to take your husband's last name are interesting, but they weren't exactly the foremost topics on my mind. I craved a place specifically for young feminists.

The problem was, I had no idea where to find that place. I resorted to Google searches. Like diving into the middle of the Pacific Ocean in search of a single, specific shell, or like scouring the plateaus of Iceland for elves (look it up), searching Google for something you're not sure even exists can be arduous and endlessly frustrating. Every once in a while, I'd find an online news site or a mainstream blog that covered the topic of sexting or teen pregnancy (always something alarmist—pregnancy pacts!—and usually focused on the threat to our one and only virtue: purity, of course). In these instances, teens would show up in the comments sections, rearing to add their two cents. But where did we have a chance to write our *own* posts? Did we have an opportunity to offer our own perspectives, not just respond to someone else's? Did our insights ever get a chance to temper the statistics that adults love to point to, and which are, more often than not, faulty and biased? (Aside: I think Fox News straight up pulls them out of their asses.) Did a forum exist for teenagers to share their general observations and to be interviewed?

No, in fact, it didn't. So I decided to create that place.

I'll admit it: When I first started blogging, I had no idea what the hell I was doing. But I definitely had a vision. I had a goal. I wanted to create a place where teens who identified as feminist—or who at least cared about feminist issues—could not only gather and find each other, but could also tell the world our *own* stories. I wanted to give every teen—feminist or not—the opportunity to speak out and have her (or his) voice heard.

Thus, the FBomb was born, and a few months later, tens of thousands of people were reading the very words I had written on caffeine-fueled late-night word-vomit binges and after fury-inducing high school/life experiences. And soon readers started to submit rants of their very own.

But more than any post about birth control, more than any feminist's personal "coming out" story, the most feminist aspect of the FBomb is its function as a platform for teen voices to be heard. In response to a culture that encourages us to be shallow drones, the FBomb is about empowering teens to use their voices, letting them know that their voices matter, and showing them that they're not alone in their feminist ideals. It's about elevating the voices of a generation—and hopefully, the continuation of a movement. It's about showing the world that feminism doesn't have to be discovered when we first face discrimination or violence or what have you. It's about showing the world that feminism is for life—from the womb to the grave. (Yes, I said "womb." I have always advocated for pregnant mothers to read feminist texts to their children while they are in utero. It's far superior to playing classical music, no matter what your ob-gyn says. Trust me: I'm a *teen feminist*, I know this stuff.)

It can be hard to really explain feminism to our peers. The FBomb is a way to *show* them. On the FBomb, teen girls wittily write about their lives. They offer each other advice in the comments. They therapeutically rant, they write short stories and contemplate current events. They're brilliant and wonderful. Feminism, for the FBomb generation, is not scary or intimidating. It's personal. Sometimes it's funny, sometimes it's depressing, sometimes it's enraging. But it's always interesting.

The FBomb is ultimately about showing young women and girls that they too can choose feminism—and that if they do, they will never be alone. It's about showing teens how being a feminist can help them, in plentiful and unexpected ways. After all, it helped me.

In addition to everything the FBomb does for its readers and contributors, it does something else. It serves as evidence (to adults, to the media, to the world at large) that teen girls want equality. That we don't want to be limited to stereotypes. That we want a real, productive way to talk about our life experiences— everything from our bodies, to hooking up, to the injustices happening in the world around us that make us feel powerless. We want all of these things, whether or not we even recognize that this *is feminism* or not.

For all that, the FBomb has been great.

But we need something more. Something like a book. A book

written by a young feminist for other young feminists, and for young men and women who don't yet know that they are feminists. A book that is brutally honest and that captures our feelings, frustrations, and opinions about the real world we are living in, right now—a world that is more than a little f'd up. We need something like *this* book.

My hope is that *A Little F'd Up* contributes to the start of a new movement. Our movement. Feminism that is relevant to *us*, the youth of today. My hope is that it brings us a step closer to truly addressing, combating, and changing all of the crap in our lives and in the lives of others that we're really freaking sick of.

This is our feminism, and there's nothing f'd up about it.

PART ONE

THE BADASSES WHO CAME BEFORE US:

A BRIEF HISTORY OF FEMINISM

I know what you're thinking: History is boring.

Actually, I have no idea if that's what you're thinking. Maybe you opened this book to this page and thought, *You mean I get another opportunity to explore the interconnecting relationships and themes of the people and events of years past and relate them to my current state, both personal and political? And outside of the confines of an academic classroom no less? Well aren't I the luckiest!?* Somehow, though, I think not. At least, I know that's not what I would've thought had this book been authored by somebody else and I were a reader. But hear me out.

There are three major reasons I think it's really important to understand the history of the women who came before us before we delve into all the shit we're dealing with right now (let alone tackling the inevitable crapstorm that's yet to come).

Reason #1:
Our generation desperately needs some perspective.

No, seriously. If I hear one more girl wonder aloud if *Roe v. Wade* was a boxing match that was recently televised by ESPN, I'm going to freakin' rip my hair out. Our ignorance is embarrassing and insulting and will only hurt us in the long run. We need to get our shit together.

Reason #2: History repeats itself and all that jazz.

I don't know if this was just my experience, but every first day of school of my entire high school career, my history teacher would saunter into class and ask us, "So, why do we need to learn about history?" Some smartass always retorted, "We don't," then probably mentally high-fived himself (it was always a "him") for his ridiculously witty response. Then, somebody would raise their hand and appease the teacher by saying, "So we don't repeat our mistakes."

Stock answer to first-day of history class or not, I really think this is true. If we don't truly understand the feminist movement—if we don't really understand what it used to be like to be a woman in this world up until not so long ago—I honestly feel like we're going to get complacent. We will be lazy about enforcing our rights, and I fear history truly will repeat itself . . . and, frankly, as women, we'll be fucked.

Reason #3: It makes sense to start at the beginning.

Yeah, this one is pretty self-explanatory. So without further ado, let's talk about the history of feminism!

BEFORE THERE WERE WAVES:
LIFE BEFORE FEMINISM

We tend to dehumanize people who lived a long time ago, viewing their faceless, nameless existence the same way we might contemplate the Big Bang theory. It's hard to see them as anything more than an abstract concept. But we must remember: It was their lives and their actions that led to our current reality.

And actually, there is less separating us from the past than we might think. Sure, Babylonians lived almost two thousand years before Jesus came along, but, as you'll see below, their treatment of women was pretty enduring. So enduring, in fact, that women's right to own property was not won in America until the first wave of feminism, thousands of years later. Though honor, virginity, and purity are no longer intrinsic to a woman's survival, as they were in ancient times, those concepts are still deeply woven into our society's perception of women, and still deeply affect our lives. And, like in ancient times, women are still sold into slavery, via human and sex trafficking. It's happening at this very moment.

It's true: We have made strides that women before us could never have comprehended. But just because we have Facebook, frozen yogurt, and, you know, the ability to *vote* doesn't mean we're done.

Prehistoric Gender Equality (Yes, It's a Thing)

If we go back—before Freud, before Shakespeare, even before Plato—we can get a glimpse of gender equality. But we have to go way back. Like, get your clubs out and try to hone your cave-painting skills, because we're going back to the very beginning.

It's believed that up until about 10,000 BC, men and women were considered equal in status. Men were primarily hunters and women primarily gatherers, but inferiority didn't factor into these roles, and women could be hunters if they were capable.[1] And then along came the Neolithic Revolution, when humans gave up the nomadic lifestyle, settled down into homes and communities, and started to develop civilizations. Only then did women get the bump.[2]

So what happened? Well, this new settled lifestyle resulted in that pesky division of labor: men as hunters, women as gatherers.

In addition to cultivating crops, women were responsible for child-bearing. Fair enough. After all, women were the ones with the uteruses and breast milk, and foraging allowed them to stay close to their responsibilities at home. Men—because of their better eyesight in dim light and their sharper hearing—stuck to hunting and, once we started domesticating animals, to herding and husbandry. It was an essentially equitable division of labor that was based on each gender's specific physical capacities.[3]

But somehow things took a sinister turn, and the division of labor came to be understood as the demarcation of a social hierarchy. Women were kept busy with numerous domestic responsibilities while their male counterparts' sole duty was tending to the flocks. Men had time to think critically, form political infrastructures, and ultimately, network with other men. Meanwhile, women were kept too busy to notice that somewhere along the line, they had become inferior.[4]

This is approximately when shit hit the fan.

Hammurabi's Uncivil Code of Conduct

Imagine you're in Babylon, a city-state in Mesopotamia. It's 1786 BC. Violence is on the rise as the leaders of your city-state are attempting to conquer everything within their reach. You can't even go to the temple to worship Shamash, the sun god, without worrying about getting shanked. It's a problem, and Hammurabi, the king, knows it. Thus, he decides to make some laws.

This is where the Code of Hammurabi comes in. A charming document, this set of 282 laws was enacted to regulate Babylonian society, and it makes the laws of most modern cultures seem like they were designed by a hippie commune. Essentially, the Code of Hammurabi decreed that there were two types of women: those who were slaves (with a master, and with absolutely no rights whatsoever), and those who were not.

Now, you might think that the nonslave women had it easy compared to the slave women—after all, they weren't bound to physical labor, right?

Okay. But that's where it ended. Because in reality, "free" women were just unofficial slaves.

Basically, the life of the "free" Babylonian woman boiled down to this:

1. You are born to your father, who owns you.

2. When you are married off, you are sold to your husband, like an animal, or a nice hat.

3. Your role in life is to have babies. *Boy* babies. Give birth to daughters, and you are on the express train to servitude. Why? Sons were the heirs. They carried on the family name and brought honor to their families, while girls drained their families of already limited resources, just to leave them and join another family once they were of marrying age. Son preference wasn't just based in sexism—it was also financial.

Women were also used as a way to settle accounts. (How convenient is it when the woman who has borne your children can also be used as collateral!) Yes, it's true: Selling off your female was the Babylonian answer to *Your 60-Second Guide to Getting Out of Debt.*[5]

As long as she wasn't worthless, that is. A woman's financial value and marriageability was intrinsically connected to her purity and good name. So accusing a woman of fooling around was a serious matter—one with a memorable punishment if you couldn't back up your claim. The 127th law states "If anyone point the finger at [that is, slander] a sister of a god or the wife of anyone and cannot prove it, this man shall be taken before the judges, and his brow shall be marked (by cutting the skin, or perhaps the hair)."[6] Once a woman was married, however, she'd better hope her husband actually wanted to have sex with her. The mere fact of marriage did not secure a woman's honored place in Babylonian society, as the 128th law makes clear: "If a man take a woman to wife but have no intercourse with her, this woman is no wife to him."[7] So as you can see, a Babylonian woman's worth and status in life depended significantly on her sex life (if you can call it that, which, no, I don't think you can).

Aristotle: Master of Politics, Astronomy, and Sexism

One can only imagine what Aristotle's mother was thinking when she first laid eyes on him. Maybe her mother's intuition allowed her to foresee the astounding contributions he would make to almost every major sphere of the Western world. Or maybe, as the wife of a physician in 384 BC, she was simply ecstatic that she gave birth to a son, which was one of the most honorable things a woman could do at the time. Either way, Aristotle did little to honor his mother's gender in return for the nine months of morning sickness, swollen feet, and mood swings, and for the endless hours of labor.

At the time of Aristotle's birth, it was understood as fact

that women were inferior to men. According to religious leaders of the time, women were silly, emotional beings, unable to reason in the same way as men did, and were therefore imperfect. However, those theologians didn't really have any way to back up these claims (other than an ingrained patriarchal system and a long history of sexism, that is). So the scientists (and I use the term lightly) sought to prove their theologians right. They wanted to support their religious leaders (probably fearing the wrath of the gods otherwise) and thus were determined to discover the logical reasons behind their institutional misogyny.

Aristotle was no exception: He set out to prove female inferiority from a biological perspective. He presented the theory that woman—though superior to animals (thanks for throwing us a bone, dude!)—was really just an inferior version of man. His "proof" was along these lines: Human strength lies in heat, and since men are warmer than women, the logical conclusion is that women, with their apparently frigid blood, were defective and physically inadequate.

But his brilliance did not end there. According to Aristotle, semen was blood that had turned white because of men's hot, hot bods. He contended that semen was far superior to menstrual blood, which was imperfect semen that hadn't been cooked long enough. These conclusions led Aristotle to finally reason that the female form was a "monstrosity."[8]

As you can see, it was quite easy to make a sexist conclusion fit a sexist hypothesis. These days we have this handy-dandy thing called "the scientific method," which clearly shows how insufficient and invalid Aristotle's mode of constructing a hypothesis was. But back then, it was just how science was done, and as a result, that "science" contributed to women's ongoing oppression.

It would have been one thing if the madness had ended here—if subsequent scientists had looked at Aristotle's ridiculous assessment of women, scratched their heads, and murmured, "This is complete bullshit." But no, that is not how the story ended. It continued for quite some time after Aristotle bid adieu to the temporal realm.

Galen (AD 130–200), a Greek physician and theorist, took a look at Aristotle's work and (apparently yearning for a bromance that could never be) decided to adopt it as his own . . . with one minor adjustment. He pointed out that the female genitals are really just an inside-out version of a male's and are therefore half-baked and inferior.[9] (Apparently, declaring menstrual blood to be undercooked semen was not sufficiently graphic or inane.)

And the madness continued on into the time of Saint Thomas Aquinas (1225–74), who perpetuated these absolutely ridiculous theories. Aquinas, however, took a look at the ole Bible, which said God could not make anything less than a perfect world, including *all* of the people who live in it. After having a brief "Oh shit!" moment, Aquinas adjusted his handy little hypothesis, stating that women, like men, were perfect. Of course they were: God had created a perfect world full of perfect people. The catch was that women were *less* perfect than men. *How could this be?* people with fully functioning brains might wonder. *How can one be "less" perfect than somebody else while still being perfect?* Well, thankfully, Aquinas had an answer: Women were mandated by God to do less-perfect work than men in the context of an altogether perfect world. What's even sadder than this pathetic explanation is that people actually bought it.[10]

Muhammad Was a Feminist (No, Seriously, I Mean It)

In the Western world, it's often taken for granted that the Muslim way of handling gender issues is far inferior to our own. "At least women can drive here," we say as we shrug our shoulders at discrimination against women in the workplace. Or we think of

BIBLICAL BADASSES

Despite the fact that women have made up roughly half of the global population since Adam and Eve/the original spin of the wheel of Samsara/the Big Bang/zombie aliens manifested planet Earth and spawned human life forms (I support all beliefs!), it's quite difficult to find badass women role models of years past. Actually, it's hard enough to find any historical women who did anything at all. Yeah, humankind (mankind, I could go so far to say) has really done a thorough job of both stifling women's societal contributions and covering up the existence of women who broke through that barrier.

If there is one place where women do abound and even have influence, however, it's the number-one summer reading pick of Focus on the Family, Opus Dei, and, if I had to guess, the Gun Owners of America: the Holy Bible.

Prisca/Priscilla:
Wife of Aquila, Gospel Spreader, BFF of Paul

Priscilla is best known for the work she and her husband, Aquila, did with the apostle Paul, spreading the good word of Christianity. Priscilla and Aquila both traveled with Paul, and they were both with him when he wrote to the Corinthians. While the Bible never comes out and says it, she was clearly more than your average biblical-era wifey. In half of the references to her and Aquila, Priscilla is mentioned *first*—indicating a relative level of importance. Not only was Priscilla respected in her vocation, but she's also an example of a strong lady finding her calling and sticking to it—something we can all admire.

Queen of Sheba:
Possibly Queen of Ancient Yemen, Woman of Action

The Queen of Sheba was clearly a take-charge kind of gal. In the Jewish version of events, she read up on King Solomon of Israel and the work he was doing, and she

→

→ was impressed. She traveled to see him and to show her approval by showering him with gifts. Also, being the saucy minx she was, she tested him with questions. He apparently passed her tests, and she rewarded him by publicly endorsing his god. Some believe she and the king were getting it on, and that she returned home with a gift of her own: the gift of life (screaming, pooping life).

In the Qur'an's version, Solomon is the one who tests the Queen of Sheba, who fails. She apologizes and ultimately submits to Solomon's god. Christianity's version went all abstract and portrayed her visit to Solomon as a metaphor for the marriage of the Church to Christ (Solomon = the Messiah; Sheba = submissive people). Neither version of the queen is quite the same feminist as the Jewish religion depicts.

Deborah:
Prophetess, and the Only Female Judge of Israel

In Deborah's time, the Israelites were leaning toward chaos (sex, drugs, rock 'n' roll), so God appointed judges to regain order. Deborah was one of them, and she was a judge who got shit done. Basically, all the male judges were wishy-washy and more interested in partying than in steering their society away from irrevocable corruption. Deborah saw this going down, rolled her eyes, and took control.

Israelites came to her to settle their disputes, and she directed men under her command, which extended to the Israeli army. In fact, Deborah led the Israelites to a victory over the Canaanites—a victory nobody saw coming because of the Canaanites' superior technology.

Mary Magdalene: Follower (and Possible Girlfriend) of Jesus and Possible Leader/Prophet/Mystic

Oh, Mary Magdalene, is there any figure in history more misunderstood than you? The Church wanted us to believe for so long that you were just a common tramp using your feminine wiles to screw with everybody. But after unearthing the Gnostic Gospels—writings that were not included in the New Testament—it seems clear that you were a *partner* of Jesus's, even though the other disciples weren't your biggest fans.

In the Bible we all know, Mary only appears long enough to make it to the cross and tomb. In reality, Mary was probably a badass chick who had as much vision and drive as good old Jesus, and yet the Church tried to cover it up. Maybe they didn't want the world to know what women were capable of, or maybe they didn't want Jesus to seem as human as he was. Either way, Mary got a bad rap.

hijabs (the head-covering worn—often by choice—by many Muslim women) as oppressive and pat ourselves on the back for being progressive . . . as we stroll past nearly naked women splayed ten stories high on massive billboards, as if it's the most normal thing in the world. Yes, it's true: In many respects, it isn't exactly easy to be a Muslim woman even today. For example, there are Muslim sects who still believe that female genital mutilation is a "sunnat" act, or one that will be rewarded in the Islam faith.[11] (However, this is a misconception: Female genital mutilation is not dictated by the Qur'an. See Part Five for more.) But I think Western cultures have a lot of self-examining to do before we claim that the entire religion of Islam is inherently sexist, and that therefore our culture is superior.

Consider the fact that while Muhammad was doing things like granting women property rights circa AD 600, Western culture still didn't have our act together almost a thousand years later, during a supposed period of "enlightenment" (see the next section).

The religion of Islam teaches that men and women are equal before God. (At the time of its inception, around AD 650, it could have been considered a radically feminist religion!) From the beginning, Muslim women were entitled to inheritance, property rights, marriage (that is, a say in proposals), and divorce (that is, the ability to initiate them).[12]

This egalitarian outlook can be attributed to the founder of Islam himself, Muhammad. As an orphan and as the father of four daughters in a son-favoring culture, Muhammad held the roles of wife, mother, and daughter in high esteem and claimed that making each one of them happy would do wonders for your ability to get into paradise after you die. Muhammad's wife, Khadijah, was not only the person Muhammad first confided in after his revelation from God, but she was also the first convert to Islam. And though they lived in a polygamous society, Muhammad and Khadijah had a monogamous relationship.[13]

Westerners tend to view Muslims as archaic because of their perceived common practice of polygamy. In fact, the Qur'an does allow for polygamy, but it's also very clear that each wife should be treated equally. Polygamy in Islamic culture was not borne from one gross guy's selfish lust, as some assume, but rather as a result of the Battle of Uhud in AD 625, which created an abundance of Muslim widows.[14]

While Muhammad did marry several more women after Khadijah's death, those marriages were all formed for political reasons—not due to some creepy wife-lust. In fact, Muhammad surrounded himself with strong women. Aisha, one of Muhammad's later wives, played an integral role in carrying on the religion, encouraging people to live the Qur'an in the way Muhammad had. She even became an expert in medicine and pottery (you go, girl).[15]

Though Muslim society began with a rather enlightened view of women, that view has certainly eroded over time. But the main factor in its erosion was not the religion itself. Other factors—such as jockeying political groups, poverty, and illiteracy—have all contributed significantly to the oppression of Muslim women. And unfortunately, there are powerful Muslim extremists who have perverted the original intentions of the Q'uran, but the work that Muhammad did for the women of his society was important and should not be forgotten.

The Renaissance and Enlightenment (Not So Enlightened, Actually)

When you think of all the massive changes that took place during the Renaissance—a three-hundred-year period of rebirth that lasted until the seventeenth century—you'd think it'd be safe to assume that the status of women might have changed too. With its philosophy of humanism and its major scientific discoveries, you'd think it would have been a time ripe for improving the position of women.

And yet, little changed.

Per usual, women were seen as lacking in discipline, and their bodies were still blamed for the devious temptation that they elicited—which in turn threatened men's positions in the societal hierarchy and caused harm to the Very Important Work they were doing. While class did affect women's roles—many noble women were allowed to commission artwork, for example—a woman's primary duties were still to "run the household" and "produce sons."

Then in the eighteenth century, along came the Enlightenment—when all the cynics came out of the woodwork and shoved the painters and sculptors of the Renaissance out of the way. The thinkers of the Enlightenment rejected religion and pondered deep, philosophical thoughts . . . and continued to deny women basic human rights. Their husbands still owned them, and their main purpose in life was to have babies.

The Enlightenment was all about reason, but this emphasis didn't extend to women. The Enlightenment only emphasized the importance of the "public sphere," where men dominated politics, debates, the economy, and society, while women were confined to the private sphere of hearth and home, making the gender roles and expectations of the Enlightenment crystal clear.

THE FIRST WAVE: THE BROADS WHO BLAZED THE TRAIL

Everybody should have seen the first wave of feminism coming. Not just because women were getting sick of being the property of their husbands and having their legal existence absorbed into their husbands'. And no, not even just because the idea of treating women as second-class citizens and denying them basic human rights like life, liberty, and property is fundamentally wrong.

No, people should have seen it coming because how long were women really going to wear corsets, sit in their parlors, and have tea and "visit" all day? It was only a matter of time before those women looked around, looked down at the china in their hands, looked at the wives of their husbands' friends, with whom they were forced to interact on a regular basis, and said to themselves, *F@#$ this. I'm done with this shit. Mary over here is a raving lunatic, and if I have to hear about her dog Fido one more time I will actually gouge out my eyes with the knitting needles I make five tea cozies a day with. I will do it. Try me.*

Or maybe it really was just because of the whole "being treated as less than human" thing. As we've seen, before the first wave (which spanned from the nineteenth century through the early twentieth), women weren't really considered people. It's not that men gave their wives treats when they behaved or put them in a crate at night to avoid "accidents," but rather that women did not have equal civic, social, economic, political, or intellectual rights. You know, all the things that contribute to a person's full status as a functioning member of society?

MARY WOLLSTONECRAFT (1759–97)

When it came to gender equality, the Enlightenment was pretty dim, actually. There was, however, a standout champion for women's rights who emerged from that era: the British writer Mary Wollstonecraft. She is often credited for setting in motion the wheels of progressive change for women both in Europe and in the United States, where she had a huge influence on the first wave of feminism.

Many people say that Mary's grim life was a stronger argument for women's rights than her writing ever was. She faced domestic violence, maternal mortality, depression, and sexual repression, which were all common consequences of being born female in the eighteenth century.

Wollstonecraft's thoughts on sexism-based adversity are best displayed in her indisputably feminist book *A Vindication of the Rights of Woman* (1792). Here's an excerpt:

> *Women are told from their infancy, and taught by the example of their mothers, that a little knowledge of human weakness, justly termed cunning, softness of temper, outward obedience, and a scrupulous attention to a puerile kind of propriety, will obtain for them the protection of man; and should they be beautiful, everything else is needless, for, at least, twenty years of their lives. . . .*[16]

Translation: Women perpetuate the cycle of submissiveness by teaching their daughters that their very lives depend on finding a man to take care of them. And that to succeed in finding a man to protect them, they must learn to be fake and manipulative . . . unless they're drop-dead gorgeous, in which case they can just ride that out for at least twenty years.

> *I lament that women are systematically degraded by receiving the trivial attentions, which men think*

→ *it manly to pay to the sex, when, in fact, they are insultingly supporting their own superiority. It is not condescension to bow to an inferior.*[17]

Translation: Chivalry should die a painful, painful death. Yeah, it may seem that opening doors or pulling out chairs for us is just a nice thing for guys to do. But when chivalry is the *only* way men pay respect to the female gender (rather than, say, asking their opinions on a current event), it becomes insulting and is a blatant demonstration of how unequal the sexes truly are.

Man, taking her body, the mind is left to rust; so that while physical love enervates man, as being his favourite recreation, he will endeavour to enslave woman: and, who can tell, how many generations may be necessary to give vigour to the virtue and talents of the freed posterity of abject slaves?[18]

Translation: Because man's favorite thing in the world is sex, he of course wants to set things up so that he can have easy access to it at any time. That's why women are repressed and made to be submissive. But the days of this messed-up system are numbered, and there will come a day when women are freed from oppression. But still, even after that, it will take generations for women to undo the long legacy of their slave mentality, to rise to their full potential. (Thanks, society. You suck.)

It's truly amazing to look back at Wollstonecraft—a woman born about 160 years before the Nineteenth Amendment was ratified—and to see how truly progressive she was. Her work was as brave as it was essential to the development of the first wave of feminism.

The leading philosophical outlook at the beginning of the nineteenth century was based on the principles of the Enlightenment, which held that humanity is characterized by having reason, virtue, and knowledge, and that to master these qualities would be a trifecta of human accomplishment. And so when it came to women, the conventional wisdom of the nineteenth century went like this: Women are destined to be imperfect, because their virtues lay in their submission; their knowledge is based on perfecting their role of submission, not on developing their intellects. (Never mind that that society *insisted* on a submissive role for women, which therefore made it impossible for them to be "perfected.")

The first wave of feminists recognized this wasn't logic—this was ridiculousness. And that the only way out was to break free from the expectation of submission. Women needed autonomy!

Thus, feminism was born.

What Was It All About?

The first wave was all about the basics. First-wave feminists were mostly concerned with convincing everybody that:

1. Women are human, despite their ovaries.

2. Women should be educated, so that instead of reproducing and throwing the occasional dinner party, they might win a Pulitzer Prize or fly solo across the Atlantic Ocean.

The most logical way to accomplish these lofty goals, feminists reasoned, was to attempt to gain the most basic types of rights. For example, they thought it might be nice to be able to vote, so that they might have a say in the actual laws that regulated their lives. They also figured while they were at it, they might rally for the right to an equal education. Reproductive rights would be nice too.

First-wave feminists wanted equality, plain and simple. And without a political voice, an adequate education, and the ability to control their bodies, those women knew they didn't have a shot in hell at achieving it. I'm sure at the time many people thought the prospect of women achieving such things was preposterous and impossible. But it wasn't. Those women achieved all they set out to do and more. And this is how they did it.

FRANCES (FANNY) WRIGHT (1795–1852)

Wright was one of the first to say that equality would benefit everybody. Men would have better-educated, more-interesting, happier wives and daughters, and everybody's interactions (including the sexual ones) would be much improved. Besides, Wright argued, women have always led men. As she said, "Yet justly might it be made a question whether those who ostensibly govern are not always unconsciously led."[19] In other words, behind every great man is a great woman. And, she reasoned, if women had such an influence on men, wouldn't it be good to make sure that influence was coming from an educated source? She understood that men were frightened by the thought of losing power, but by imprisoning the minds of women, she argued, men's minds were also bound.[20]

Fanny was way ahead of her time. In addition to being a feminist, she was an atheist, an opponent of slavery, and an advocate for labor unions, free public education, and sexual freedom. (It's amazing people didn't run from her in fear, screaming that she was possessed by the devil.)

She was so badass, she even had a derogatory term named after her. To be a "Fanny Wrightist" was to be as far as one could possibly be beyond the scope of respectability.

And that, my friends, is the ultimate mark of success.

SOJOURNER TRUTH (1795–1883)

"Ahead of her time" doesn't even begin to cover it when it comes to Sojourner Truth. Not only was she one of the first black women to take up the feminist cause, but she was also one of the first black women to speak publicly and to be a prominent figurehead for a cause. She was the only black woman at the 1850 First National Women's Rights Convention, and she traveled across the country speaking out against slavery and sexism.

Sojourner Truth's "Ain't I a woman?" speech is easily one of the ultimate hate shutdowns of all time. At the 1851 Women's Convention in Akron, Ohio, a triad of pastors each gave his own reasoning for the superiority of men. The women attending the convention didn't even want Sojourner to speak, lest her race draw attention away from the gender issue. Sojourner verbally bitchslapped the entire audience, bringing them all back to sense by eloquently questioning the idea of what makes a woman. Here are some excerpts:

> *I could work as much and eat as much as a man— when I could get it—and bear the lash as well! And ain't I a woman? . . . . If my cup won't hold but a pint, and yours holds a quart, wouldn't you be mean not let me have my little half-measure full? . . . Then that little man in black there, he says women can't have as much rights as men, 'cause Christ wasn't a woman! Where did your Christ come from? Where did your Christ come from? From God and a woman! Man had nothing to do with Him. If the first woman God ever made was strong enough to turn the world upside down all alone, these women together ought to be able to turn it back, and get it right side up again! And now they is asking to do it, the men better let them* [21]

THE RIGHT TO VOTE

When we learn about the suffragists in school, we're always shown pictures of matronly women in their Sunday best standing rigidly and properly with immaculately printed signs.

But the thing is, those women were total badasses.

SUSAN B. ANTHONY (1820–1906)

Long before Twitter rallied the masses to fight for justice and change, Susan B. Anthony's forte was social organizing. Her claim to fame is successfully registering to vote and then voting in the federal election. She almost got away with this stunt, but the police caught her. Anthony was arrested, but being the whipsmart lady she was, she used the Fourteenth Amendment, stating that a citizen is defined as "all persons born or naturalized in the United States"—and, as a person who fit that definition of citizen, she had the right to vote. The dirtbag judge ruled that the Fourteenth Amendment was not applicable. Of course, he'd made up his mind before the trial even started and told the jury that he expected a guilty verdict out of them. And he got it.

But she delivered a killer argument at her trial. She argued that if she couldn't be considered a legal citizen (since citizens *could* vote), then she would refuse to consent to the duties of a citizen, such as paying taxes. She also called "bullshit" on the jury (who were all men of course), as they weren't her peers, nor were they unbiased.

After the guilty verdict, the judge ordered a fine of a hundred dollars. Anthony (with what I can only imagine was the definition of a withering stare) told him that though she was ten thousand dollars in debt from trying to print a newsletter about women's rights, and though she would pay back every cent of *that* debt, she would not pay a single penny of his stupid unfair fine. And so she did a little time. But she never paid that fine.

What. A. Badass.

And I don't just mean in a historical context. I mean they voted illegally. They were arrested. They endured the social repercussions for standing up for their beliefs, and they *fought* for what they believed in. Don't let the sashes and flowered hats fool you. They were freakin' warriors.

But of all the things to start the feminist movement with, why did first-wavers focus so intently on the right to vote? Why was suffrage so important?

If we consider the goal of "putting an end to a political climate of complete inequality" to be the first wave's priority, then the fact that the founding mothers of feminism were all about suffrage makes complete sense: Voting—or having a political voice—is the most obvious way to change a faulty political system. Sure, women could've begged their husbands to *pretty please* do something about the unjust way in which they were completely ignored. But doing so would have not only been demeaning, but also would have reinforced the ideas men had about women being like petulant children (and therefore, unequal). It just didn't make sense. They couldn't just ask for the right to vote—they had to demand it.

And so, the first-wavers began to organize. They founded groups, started petitions, and wrote newspapers. They spoke out, publicly and in the written word—refusing to let the world continue to believe that women had nothing valuable to say. They learned that women would always be stronger together than they ever could be apart. Finally, in 1920, the Nineteenth Amendment was ratified, and women officially had the right to vote.

Let's just take a minute to process that. Women didn't have the right to vote until 1920. We talk about that fact casually in class, and we have memorized the date for our American history tests, but I don't think we really understand the implications of that date. Less than a hundred years ago, women were valued so little that men completely excluded them from having any type of say or influence over the very structure and progress of our country. A hundred years in the context of the history of the human race is absolutely nothing.

So once you turn eighteen (or if you already are), take your right to vote seriously. Not just as a responsible adult, not just as an American citizen, but as a woman too. Because believe me, that "right" is not a given.

EQUAL EDUCATION

Also essential to achieving baseline equality was the right to equal education—the ability for women to receive an education equal to that of their male counterparts. Prior to the first wave of feminism, the prevailing belief was that women should not be educated to the same extent that men were. There were several arguments for this belief, including the argument that women weren't mentally capable of comprehending what men could, and that women were destined for a life of domesticity anyway, and so education would be useless to them.[22]

First-wave feminists were the first to call this what it really was: bullshit. They knew that women's minds were as valuable as anybody else's, and that by denying women educations, we were basically halving our progress as a culture at large. Educating women, first-wave feminists believed, was an essential component of achieving equality. The idea that women are not as intelligent as men was not rooted in fact, they argued, but rather was a product of society—and one that could be easily remedied by educating men and women equally. Feminists began to establish places of higher education for women (fun fact: Oberlin College was the first American institution to grant admission to female and black students). They also reformed girls' secondary-school system, mandating their participation in formal national exams.

FREDERICK DOUGLASS (1818–95)

Including men in feminism is and always has been an issue for the movement. But what most people don't realize is that to some extent, men have been involved in feminism from the get-go. Frederick Douglass is a perfect example of one such extraordinary man.

Born into slavery, Douglass somehow learned to read and write. He eventually escaped from bondage and began to speak about his experience as a slave. In 1845, he brilliantly reflected on the experience of slavery in his autobiography, *Narrative of the Life of Frederick Douglass, an American Slave*. Three years later, he published the first issue of the *North Star,* an abolitionist journal.

Though he is probably most remembered for his abolitionist work, Frederick Douglass was also a major supporter of women's rights. He attended the 1848 Seneca Falls Convention (the first women's rights convention), where he eloquently spoke in favor of women's suffrage. Soon after, Douglass wrote in the *North Star:*

> *All that distinguishes man as an intelligent and accountable being is equally true of woman; and if that government is only just which governs by the free consent of the governed, there can be no reason in the world for denying to woman the exercise of the elective franchise, or a hand in making and administering the laws of the land.*[23]

Douglass even cofounded the American Equal Rights Association with Elizabeth Cady Stanton and Susan B. Anthony.

So, now you know: feminism is and has always been for men too (although, generally, only really awesome, badass men).

SARAH (1792–1873) AND
ANGELINA EMILY (1805–79) GRIMKÉ

Born into a large, wealthy, Episcopalian family in South Carolina, the whipsmart Grimké sisters bristled that their brothers were allowed a full education, whereas they were allowed to study only subjects deemed appropriate for women.

One of the subjects that *was* deemed appropriate for women was Bible study. And the Grimké sisters used that to its full advantage, dropping some knowledge on the New England women who came to their public lectures. There was no distinction between men and women as "moral, intelligent beings" in God's book, they said. The Bible was not saying women aren't equal to men, they explained—that was just the way the sexist jerks had been interpreting it for so long. What might help this situation, the Grimké sisters reasoned, would be allowing women to be pastors. Yes, that's right: At the time, women were forbidden from taking the pulpit. Meanwhile, sexist assholes were perfectly welcome to indoctrinate their congregations with misogynistic sermons.

And, just like their other first-wave compatriots, the Grimkés pointed fingers at unequal education as a culprit. Because men were allowed to learn Hebrew and Greek, they could translate and interpret the Bible as they pleased. And women—who were kept illiterate in such languages—had to accept those translations and interpretations.

I think we can all agree that Sarah and Angelina Emily win the official title of "Greatest Ass-Kicking Sister Duo of All Time."

REPRODUCTIVE RIGHTS AND SEX EDUCATION

Generally, the second wave is recognized for launching the sexual revolution. But what most people don't realize is that while the second wave did do some awesome work in redefining female sexuality and taking a sledgehammer to puritanical attitudes about sex, the mothers and even the grandmothers of the second wave made some notable contributions on the sex front as well.

The first-wave reproductive rights movement was largely led by Margaret Sanger (see boxed text), who inspired her female peers

MARGARET SANGER (1879–1966)

At a time when talking about sex was seriously taboo, Margaret Sanger—the epitome of "the cool aunt"—was the first to step up and fight for contraceptives. She acknowledged that fighting for suffrage, property rights, and custodial rights was all well and good, but argued that if women couldn't shamelessly talk about something as fundamental as sexual reproduction, we'd never be truly liberated.

In addition to promoting contraceptives as a means of control (and therefore, as a means of increased opportunities) and calling for more-comprehensive sex education, Sanger also proposed the idea of unions for mothers, who needed their work to be acknowledged as socially important, not a mere gender role. And, she argued, all mothers should get health benefits. (Pregnancy and childbirth take a toll on a woman's body. Ask anyone who's done it.)

In 1916, she opened America's first birth-control clinic in Brooklyn. Within days, it was raided by the police, resulting in a monthlong prison sentence for Sanger (such a badass). But throughout her life, she worked tirelessly to promote sex-education and birth control for women of all races, classes, and stages in life.

Our generation, which has an array of birth-control options, really needs to give a shout out to Margaret Sanger.

to really take control of their sex lives. Sanger and her followers believed that *voluntary* motherhood was the true key to liberty, and that every woman should have the right to control her own body (seriously, a thousand pastors must have cast aspersions on these women's houses). They believed motherhood limits women to the specific role of caregiving, despite their obvious abilities to achieve more. But first-wave feminists also recognized that before we could even hope to have reproductive control over our bodies, we needed to have sex ed. At the time, ignorance about reproduction was mind-blowing, and birth control was, according to most, only for "jezebels."

Admittedly, Sanger and her followers approached the matter of reproductive rights in a very practical way and only discussed it in relation to how it affected our basic human rights, rather than from a more personal perspective, but still: In a time when sex was just *not talked about,* these women made it their business to make the world think about it. They spread the belief that letting women control their own bodies would automatically open up to them every other avenue (suffrage, property rights, and all that other good stuff), and ultimately, to full-on equality.

Key First-Wave Moments

Clearly, during the first wave, a lot of really awesome, badass women who were light years ahead of their time got together. They wrote petitions; they organized; they wrote impassioned essays and delivered fiery speeches. But what exactly did they accomplish?

The answer: a whole fucking lot.

NEW YORK'S MARRIED WOMEN'S PROPERTY ACT

Here's the deal. Up until 1848, a woman *did not legally exist* once she was married. (I might add that an unmarried woman didn't really exist back then either, in the sense that she was pretty much a social leper who was forced into hermithood and encouraged to get hundreds—nay, thousands—of cats.) Upon marriage, woman's legal existence was "absorbed" into her groom's—along with any real estate she happened to own.

New York's Married Women's Property Act of 1848 changed that, giving women in the state the right to own property (which, if you recall, is cited in the Declaration of Independence as a basic human right, right up there with life and liberty—so, you know, pretty important). It also gave women the right to hang on to that property once married, and to be able to acquire property while married without their husbands' being able to mess with it. (You know, in case she wanted to make some money off of it, or to just keep it in the family, rather than her husband turning it into a Victorian version of Hooters or something.)

The driving forces behind the act were Elizabeth Cady Stanton (see boxed text); Paulina Wright Davis, a suffragist and women's health advocate; and Ernestine Rose, who changed the property laws in her home country of Poland before immigrating to New York and doing the same. Of their success, Rose acknowledged that because the result would only affect moneyed women, it was significant but "not much . . . only for the favored few and not for the suffering many."[24] For the time, that was an uncharacteristically (and impressively) class-conscious statement.

THE SENECA FALLS DECLARATION

In 1848—the same year that New York's Married Women's Property Act was slam-dunked into the basket of women's rights successes—those suffragists were at it again, getting frisky in Seneca Falls, New York.

The masterminds behind the Seneca Falls Declaration of Sentiments and Resolutions—Elizabeth Cady Stanton (see boxed text) and Lucretia Mott—first met in 1840 while rallying at an abolition

ELIZABETH CADY STANTON (1815–1902)

One of the few (or only) names high school students can remember after studying the women's rights movement in U.S. history is "Elizabeth Cady Stanton." Her name is remembered for good reason—most notably, her leadership in the Seneca Falls Convention and her influential writing. She was also a major player in ensuring the passage of New York's Married Women's Property Act.

In her writing, Stanton emphasized how society would only benefit by allowing its best members—regardless of gender—to lead and have voices. She pointed out the fact that while men were defined by their ability to lead and by the validity of their thoughts and opinions, women were defined by their ability to fulfill other people's needs (read: wifely duties). This veritable servitude was poisonous, she reasoned, and the only antidotes were self-reliance and autonomy. We're all just human, she reasoned, and it sucks to be all of us (a cynic after my own heart!), so can't we all just make the human condition a little easier by allowing each one of us the freedom to reach our full potential?

convention. Ironically, this antislavery convention was discriminating against women. Somehow, the guys had no problem with demanding human rights for a marginalized race while simultaneously denying them from the marginalized gender.

Well, Stanton and Mott were having nothing of it. The two got their shit together and eight years later, in 1848, came up with the Seneca Falls Declaration. Basically, they rewrote the Declaration of Independence the way it should have been written the first time: with gender equality central to the text. (Some might call this plagiarism; I call it an effective rhetorical model used to incite social change.) In their version of the Declaration of Independence, the Seneca gals added twelve resolutions. Here's a rundown:

* Any laws that conflict with women's overall happiness have got to go.

* Laws that enforce female inequality or inferiority within society must also go.

* Women and men are equal. God knows it, society demands it, deal with it.

* Ignorance is no longer an excuse: Women must be educated on their legal rights (and, you know, some other stuff, like math and whatnot, while we're at it).

* Women should be able to speak publicly and teach, especially in religious communities.

* No more double standards: The same "virtue, delicacy, and refinement of behavior" applied to women also needs to be applied to men.

* No more opposition to women speaking in public. They have every right to be speaking, and they've got some damn good things to say.

* Men's interpretations of the Bible, in addition to good ole sexism, confines women to the domestic sphere, whereas they deserve to be in *all* spheres. That's what's up.

* Women deserve to vote. Because anything less is just bullshit.

* Equality should be determined by one's "capabilities and responsibilities," not by gender. In other words, really dumb men are equal to really dumb women (or, if we're going to be all positive about it, really smart women are equal to really smart men).

* Women should be able to teach, write, or speak on behalf of causes important to them.

* Women *and* men need to promote these resolutions and fight for women's rights. We're all in this together.

MARGARET FULLER (1810–50)

Like the Grimké sisters, Ms. Fuller was at the forefront of the movement of women fighting both for women's rights and for the abolition of slavery. In addition to being an author, she was one of the first female editors of prominent periodicals such as *The Dial* and the *New York Tribune*.

Fuller was known for her "conversations" for women—Socratic seminars that encouraged women of all walks of life to think critically and philosophically about the world around them. In these seminars, and in her writings, Fuller questioned the ideas (seen at the time as social fact) that women's involvement in politics was unseemly, and that women shouldn't be allowed to speak in public or assume leadership roles in their religions. Women thirst for such involvement, Fuller argued. Stimulation is a human desire—not one felt by men and men alone. The fact that women were getting together and chewing over philosophical dilemmas reached well past what was expected of the domestic sphere.

In her own time, Margaret Fuller was an inspirational thought-leader, and she continued to be a major inspiration for feminists for years to come.

THE NINETEENTH AMENDMENT: THE RIGHT TO VOTE

In 1848, the Seneca Falls convention and the Declaration of Sentiments and Resolutions got the ball rolling. But things really kicked into gear when Susan B. Anthony got in on the suffragist action at the 1852 Women's Rights Convention in Syracuse, New York. By then, it was officially decided: Women really needed the right to vote. Like *now*.

Thus, in 1878—after years of political and social activism on behalf of the suffragist cause—the following amendment was proposed:

Section 1: The right of citizens of the United States to vote shall not be denied or abridged by the United States or by any State on account of sex.

SUSAN B. ANTHONY & ELIZABETH CADY STANTON: AN IM CONVERSATION

SuzieB.A.: holy shit liz you'll never believe what I just did

GirlsRock1871: what?!

SuzieB.A.: i just voted, that's what's up!

GirlsRock1871: no freakin way!

SuzieB.A.: way! some democrats were gettin all pissy but then this one republican dude was like "let her put her vote in the box man!" and his friend was all like "yeah we'll fight you if you don't!"

GirlsRock1871: oh man, wish i coulda been there! were the republican guys cute?

SuzieB.A.: so not the point. seriously, we finally voted! it's about time! we're half the population and we deserve a say

GirlsRock1871: damn straight

SuzieB.A.: somebody at the door brb

SuzieB.A.: crap it's the police! GIRL POWER PEACE OUT!!!

Section 2: Congress shall have power to enforce this article by appropriate legislation.

So basic. So innocuous. And yet the amendment had to be introduced in every session of Congress for the next *forty-one years* before it was passed. Some progress was made in the meantime: Several individual states and territories were ahead of the game and gave women the right to vote, and in 1912, Theodore Roosevelt's political party openly supported women's suffrage. But it wasn't until 1919 (again, *forty-one years* later) that the amendment was passed by Congress. It was ratified in July 1920.

It took a few decades of persuasion, but those saucy first-wavers eventually got their way.

THE SECOND WAVE
(AND THE LEGENDARY BURNING OF THE BRAS)

The first wave fought for legal, economic, and intellectual equality and was largely successful. Women gained the right to property, custody of their children, and, perhaps most importantly, the right to vote.

But after the euphoria wore off, it was clear that more work needed to be done. Ladies and gentlemen, I give you the second wave of feminism.

What's It All About?

Yes, the first wave kicked political ass. But here's the thing: Something can be written as law, but very often, the implementation is half-assed. Legislative progress (such as the kind that was made in the first wave) might *imply* change, but, as feminists soon found out, achieving social and cultural equality is another thing entirely.

Achieving *that* kind of equality thus became the duty of the second wave. Basically, second-wave feminism sought to understand and fight oppression in addition to continuing the quest for equality.

So how does a group of people seek to achieve social and cultural equality? Legal equality, though it was certainly difficult to accomplish, was more or less clear-cut. You fought for a law to be implemented, and it either was or was not. How can a group of people change the way society at large behaves and thinks? How can we even know whether or not such a pursuit is working?

Second-wave feminists sought to address these problems in several ways. First, they decided that women would have to work together—they would have to form a sisterhood. They also determined that that sisterhood really had to include *everybody*, which meant addressing issues of race and class, among other social identifiers. They aimed to get women to communicate honestly with other women, as well as with themselves. They also sought to win even more legal rights (yeah, believe it or not, the first wave didn't win every legal right possible for women).

"SISTERHOOD IS POWERFUL"

In a perfect world, girls and women would unconditionally support each other. We'd recognize our similarities, try to understand our differences, and use this knowledge to form unbreakable bonds.

However, the real world isn't exactly like this. Any girl who has been a freshman in high school and has interacted with senior girls knows this. Any girl who has been hazed on a sports team or in a sorority knows this. Any girl who has crushed on a guy who was taken and made it a little too obvious *really* knows this. Girls don't always look at other girls and see them as "one of their own."

This is probably because half the world is women. Yes, gender divides the world in half, and gender is a huge source of half the world's oppression. But unlike members of most oppressed groups, who tend to stick together, we women don't utilize our commonality to bond with every other member of our gender. We instead form groups based on an array of other factors.

Second-wave feminism sought to change this with the concept of "sisterhood," or "solidarity founded on shared experiences of oppression."[25] In fact, sisterhood was so important during the second wave that "Sisterhood Is Powerful" was a major slogan of the entire movement.

Why? Well, culture at the time was structured in a way that isolated women. They lived on the tiny islands of their homes and felt that there was nothing more for them, because they weren't able to confer with anybody who would tell them any different. As a result of second-wave sisterhood, women began to experience

GLORIA STEINEM (1934–)

Ms. Steinem was the Playboy Bunny Hugh Hefner wished he never hired.

That's right: This major second-wave feminist got her start as a journalist by going undercover as a Playboy Bunny when those nasty-ass Playboy Clubs, where young women dressed up in bunny costumes and served drinks to "key holders" were all the rage. (Long live chauvinists and their weird exclusive clubs!) She then went on to cofound *Ms.* magazine, the Ms. Foundation for Women, Choice USA, and the Women's Media Center. In her spare time, she traveled the country lecturing on women's rights, campaigned for the Equal Rights Amendment, and worked on behalf of pro–labor union organizations.

But before kicking all that ass, she was a conformist. In her 1972 essay "Sisterhood," she admits she used to brag about being told she "writes like a man," that she eschewed women's groups, and that she accepted sexism as part of our own and other cultures. But then she had a "click" moment—a realization of why feminism was important and relevant to her own life. She realized

their "click" moments together; to join together in the comfort that women understand things about each other that men never will. And thus it became easier for women to form identities around each other, rather than around the men in their lives. Because of sisterhood, newly empowered women took action, knowing they weren't alone—their sisters had their backs.

Second-wave feminists identified three important reasons why sisterhood is powerful.

1. Sisterhood helps identify the problems.

If we're all silent and keep our problems to ourselves, we'll never realize that we're not alone in our suffering. Feminists believe that

that despite the fact that men and women are equal, men exploit differences—primarily physical differences—in order to accomplish "economic and social profit of patriarchy."[26] When she realized this, Gloria put her foot down and started to protest the patriarchy.

Some of her greatest writing can be found in her book of essays *Outrageous Acts and Everyday Rebellions.* To take one example, in her essay "In Praise of Women's Bodies," Steinem examines the male "locker room" culture, in which men can bond and be comfortable with their bodies, whereas women aren't allowed to bond with our bodies and are forced to compete with each other.

Gloria Steinem is a feminist rockstar. No, seriously: Most feminists become total fangirls at even the briefest mention of her name. But unlike the many rockstars who are all hype, Steinem is the real deal and totally deserving of our adoration. A brilliant and prolific writer, an incredible public speaker, and an inspiration to all, Steinem was essential to the progress made by second-wave feminists, and she continues to do wonderful work today.

bitchfests are not only cathartic, but are also absolutely necessary for the advancement of our status as women. (So next time you're maniacally ranting to your best friend, realize you're doing the world a favor.)

For example, if we never started talking to each other about what was pissing us off, we never would have made strides against sexual harassment. Before women started talking to each other about how demeaned they felt when men on the street hollered "Nice ass, baby" (or worse) at them, or how uncomfortable they felt at work because of that creepy asshole Steve, sexual harassment was just accepted—either as a "compliment" (seriously?) or as something women had to just deal with.

(Related movie: *9 to 5,* starring Dolly Parton, Lily Tomlin, Jane Fonda, and Dabney Coleman. Earn bonus points by watching it with your mom.)

2. Sisterhood helps us raise awareness.

Bonding as sisters and creating groups can also help us spread information about the feminist cause, especially to other women who wouldn't otherwise have access. For example, by forming consciousness-raising groups, feminists can offer a shoulder to lean on, not to mention substantive support after a woman has faced some sort of adversity, like sexual harassment at work or an abusive relationship. They can confirm that such instances are not okay and can encourage each other to incite change—in their own lives and in society at large.

So next time you're out with your girlfriends, feel free to drop some feminist knowledge into the conversation.

FOR EXAMPLE:

Beatrice: I really love Ted, but he's always reading my text messages and logging on to my Facebook and reading my inbox messages. I just feel like I have no privacy. Also he uses way too much Axe and he got a Beiber-cut and—

Hester: Dude, Beatrice, wait. That's actually *not* a healthy relationship. Let me tell you about what I just learned from this awesome feminist book about healthy relationships.

Bam. Feminist consciousness-raising for the win.

3. Sisterhood just feels damn good.

In school, it's easy to lose sight of the concept of sisterhood outside your group of best friends. And sometimes, when your group is warring against another group (Why? Did she steal your friend's boyfriend? Did she call your other friend fat? Do you even remember?), it can be easy to get caught up in the drama and condemn another girl as "the enemy."

Sometimes we might even think that taking another girl down a peg will make us feel better. (Come on, we've all walked past some girl at school and thought *Well at least I don't look like* that *today—* and got high off our sense of superiority.)

But in reality, actually interacting in healthy and supportive ways with each other will make us feel way better than that. Don't believe me? Give it a try. Give a fellow female a random compliment. The way they react (if they aren't like "Who the hell are you?"—which, believe me, happens sometimes, but whatever) will make your day.

There are no downfalls to the sisterhood, and we have so much to gain by being a part of it. The second wave understood this and drew strength from it. It's about time we start doing what's needed to truly carry on that legacy.

RACE AND CLASS

Apart from a few notable names (such as Sojourner Truth and Frederick Douglass), the first wave of feminism was mostly fought by white middle- to upper-class women. The second wave still catches a lot of flak for catering to that same demographic. After all, the birth of the movement did largely come from Betty Friedan's book *The Feminine Mystique,* which focused on middle-class housewives who were depressed because they were really freakin' bored and resented their kids (what many people considered to be "white-people problems").

That said, there were second-wavers who realized that the issues of race and class were central to the feminist cause. They understood that if they were going to fight for equality, they had to fight for equality for *everyone.* These feminists sought to dispel the notion that inferiority and superiority had anything to do with race. They also insisted that a person's class is not a function of effort or laziness, but a byproduct of a rigid social structure that favors people who already have power. They looked at how oppression intersects not just with gender but also with class, race, disability, and sexuality, and they understood that *all of these factors* were relevant to achieving progress in equality and liberation.

Nevertheless, the second wave wasn't completely devoid of racism and classism. And even today, the prominent voices of the movement come from white middle- and upper-class women. And the fact is, though second-wave feminism did promote the idea of sisterhood, issues of race and class complicated that idea, and continue to do so today. After all, the majority of the world's women aren't white and aren't middle- to upper-class. The majority of us aren't *only* faced with sexism, but with classism and racism too. And if that majority senses that the white, well-off women leading the show don't understand the complicated reality of their struggles, it creates a serious divide, when we might instead be fighting the good fight together.

In 2008, I had the great honor of interviewing Gloria Steinem (see boxed text) for the FBomb. When the subject of racism came up, she made an excellent point:

> Actually, in the long term, it's not possible to be a feminist without being antiracist, and it's not possible [to be] antiracist without also being a feminist. The most obvious reason is that most women in the world are not white. But also, if you look at the cultures that are the most egalitarian so far, [they] are one-race cultures— say, Scandinavian countries, or matrilineal cultures in Africa and Asia—because the added motive of racism isn't there. If you want to maintain a racist structure, you have to maintain some *visible* difference. To do that, you have to control whom white women have children with. So these two caste systems are just enmeshed; you really can't defeat them one at a time.[27]

ALICE WALKER (1944-)

A celebrated African American author, poet, and activist, Alice Walker grew up in a poor family of Georgia sharecroppers living under Jim Crow laws. Her parents struggled hard to provide her with an education, and she graduated at the top of her class, earning a full scholarship to Spelman College in Atlanta. Later, she transferred to Sarah Lawrence College in New York. But while she was at Spelman, she was inspired to become a civil-rights activist, both as a result of Howard Zinn (her professor at the time) and by a meeting with Dr. Martin Luther King, Jr. during his visit to the college.

Alice Walker was one of the first feminists to examine the intersection of race issues with gender issues. Her creative work (such as her Pulitzer Prize–winning novel, *The Color Purple*) consistently deals with racism, sexism, and violence, and she has emerged over time as a voice for women of color in the feminist movement. In her book *In Search of Our Mother's Gardens,* she coined the term "womanism" to describe the experiences of women of color in terms of feminism—a response, in part, to what many viewed as their marginalization within the mainstream feminist movement.

Her gift with words has made its mark over the years. One powerful and oft-cited Alice Walker quote is "The most common way people give up their power is by thinking they don't have any." Well worth remembering.

Feminism's relationships with race and class are obviously complicated, and have been so since the beginning of the movement. It's important to acknowledge this, as upsetting and embarrassing as it might be. But in the end, we must accept our roots, learn from our mistakes, and look toward a brighter future.

"THE PERSONAL IS POLITICAL"

This phrase was the battle cry of the second wave. Basically, what it meant was that women had suffered privately for far too long. Before the second wave, women didn't consider their personal problems (everything from lack of personal fulfillment to double standards) to be significant. They kept their problems, their pain, and their opinions to themselves. They told themselves that such repression was just part of being a woman.

The second-wave feminists told these women—and the rest of the world—that the issues they faced in daily life needed to be inserted into the public sphere, where they could be discussed, considered, and solved. Oppression wasn't limited only to women's economic or political existence; it pertained to their social existence as well.

Women were largely excluded from the public sphere and confined to the private (read: domestic) sphere—cooking, cleaning, raising the kids, the whole shebang. This meant they were excluded from public debate about the issues that most affected their lives. Women were like "WTF?" and realized that it was time to get the heck out of their ~~jails~~ houses and do some work out there in the real world.

The slogan "The Personal Is Political" helped women in two major ways:

1. It made them realize that their personal problems were not only valid, but were also the result of big political problems.

2. It showed women that confronting their personal problems was a hugely important political act.

INTERNALIZED OPPRESSION

During the second wave, women looked around and realized that the socially accepted perception of women *sucked*. Upon further

BETTY FRIEDAN (1921–2006)

A Smith College graduate, Friedan studied journalism, just like her mother—who was never able to pursue a career because of marriage and children. Friedan refused to end her career completely after marrying, having children, and moving to the suburbs. But even so, she felt unfulfilled.

Interested in getting to the root of such feelings, Friedan created a survey that she sent to fellow Smith graduates. Two hundred women replied, revealing that they too felt unfulfilled. When a variety of women's magazines refused to publish Friedan's articles on the subject, she decided to turn the project into a full-fledged book. Thus in 1963, *The Feminine Mystique*—and essentially, the second wave of feminism—was born. (For more about the book, see the section called *The Feminine Mystique*).

But her work didn't stop when she put down the pen. She went on to cofound the National Organization for Women (NOW) and the National Women's Political Caucus. As a major advocate for the Equal Rights Amendment and abortion rights, Friedan worked tirelessly as an activist for the majority of her life.

analysis, it was discovered that there is a devastating three-step process in which society effectively keeps women subjugated by psychologically convincing them to hold themselves back (a.k.a. "internalized oppression"). Here's how it works:

Step 1: Stereotyping

Think of the words often used to describe women: "attractive," "caring," "nurturing," "quiet," "passive," "bad at math." Women are put into a box, where they are supposed to adhere to these qualities, (which, in the scheme of power, don't get us anywhere). With these qualities, we sure can soothe a screaming child (and who among us doesn't aspire to wipe boogers from a wailing toddler's nose?), but becoming CEO of a Fortune 500 company is probably out of the question. Instead of seeing women as singular individuals, all women are conflated into one singular cultural perception of women. This is called "stereotyping."

Step 2: Mystification

When we begin to believe that the stereotype is fact, and therefore start to view ourselves in terms of abstract ideals instead of as unique individuals, we've fallen prey to "mystification." This is debilitating in all kinds of ways. If our main concern is being slim, attractive, ageless, flawless, and desirable, then everything else (such as education, career, creativity, you name it) falls by the wayside. We become not only weaker, but also incomplete as human beings.

Step 3: Sexual Objectification

Once women can be packaged into nice little boxes with labels, it becomes easy to view them more as objects than as people. And in a material world, what are objects for, if not for making life more pleasant? When society routinely ignores women's unique personalities, specific emotions, and vast capacity to think, it's easy to see them as serving one purpose and one purpose only. (I'll give you a hint as to what that purpose is: It's not astrophysics.)

In these three easy steps, girls start to internalize oppression. Expecting girls to be less than who they are shapes their self-perception and creates a diminished self-image. In other words, they believe the lie, and they take it for reality. And they act accordingly. This doesn't just start and end with a cameramen from *Girls Gone Wild* asking girls to take their shirts off. It's in the little stuff too—and maybe that more than anything. When we use male-preferring language (like male-gendered pronouns for neutral words), we're sending out a clear message: "Men are the default gender. Women are just 'the others.'" It might not seem like The Most Sexist Act of All Time. But there's no disputing that language affects our understanding of the world and shapes who we are.

The women of the second wave stood up and pointed out the phenomenon of internalized oppression. They fought hard to raise our awareness of these invisible chains with the hope that we would eventually break free of them.

EMBODIMENT

Just as women's personalities and capabilities are stereotyped and objectified, our bodies are often subjected to society's control as well.

Second-wave feminists had a problem with this and sought to change it. They examined how people live in their bodies, and how our bodies shape who we are. They realized that instead of letting society victimize us through our bodies, we could use our bodies to our advantage and as a positive force in the world. Feminists urged women to explore, embrace, and claim ownership of their own bodies. For example, second-wave feminists launched this little thing called the sexual revolution, in which they taught other women that they deserved sexual satisfaction and had the right to express their sexuality just as much as men.

The second wave made great contributions to raising awareness about eating disorders, female sexuality, sexual violence, and beauty standards, just to name a few things, and took the necessary first steps toward helping women develop better relationships with their bodies.

Key Achievements of the Second Wave

Our second-wave grandmas probably look at us and see a bunch of young women who have reaped the benefits of their hard work and used it to become a band of texting fiends who just can't decide between the sparkly vampire or the buff werewolf.

And to some extent, they do have a right to be pissed off. We do take our rights for granted (as evidenced by all the girls who join Facebook groups like "I give women respect. LOL jk, make me a sandwich bitch!" and think they're hilarious). So it's only right that we at least try to understand what those second-wavers did for us. The truth is, we could barely do anything before they came along.

Believe it or not, because the second wave got Title IX passed, we are one of the first generations of women to be able to play sports at high school and college levels. Oh, and if you were a pre-second-wave girl who had hopes of growing up to be a scientist, a mathematician, or a CEO, you were living in an imaginary world. No, your options were as follows: secretary, teacher, nurse, or baby-machine—although the Pill was not legal yet, so baby-machine wasn't really "optional."

Before the second wave, women pretty much worked just as a way to kill time until they got married—or as a great way to meet their future husbands (that is, if they hadn't already done so in college, which was also seen as a way of procuring hubbies—as long as you didn't make the mistake of getting too educated, which would just scare all the boys away). Of course, you could always skip the whole college/work thing and settle down in your late teens and start having babies right away. And if you chose that route, nobody would criticize you for "throwing your life away" like they would these days. Instead, people would just be like, "Oh good, getting a head start there, I see?"

THE PILL

Ever wonder what women did before they had the Pill? It wasn't pretty. Not to get graphic, but let's just say that in preindustrial America, "herbs" and "elixirs" were used both to the prevent pregnancy and to induce miscarriages—definitely not ideal options.[28]

In 1952, at age seventy-two, leading feminist Margaret Sanger

THE BRA-BURNING THAT NEVER WAS

In 1968, the blossoming women's liberation movement decided it was time to make some very public waves. And what better venue was there than the Miss America Pageant: the epitome of female objectification and televised nationwide to millions of viewers?

And so second-wave feminists successfully stole the spotlight from their pageant-participating counterparts. They made some waves, for sure. The only problem is that instead of being remembered for making a bold statement about reclaiming their bodies, most people recall this incident as "the time those anarchist man-haters burned their bras." *Sigh.*

Yes, I'm sorry to disappoint, but the truth is feminists never actually burned their bras at that rally. Actually setting fire to their undergarments would have been a fire-hazard (safety first!). So along with some girdles, mops, pots and pans, and *Playboy* magazines (all of which they called "instruments of female torture"), they threw their bras into garbage cans (which, again, *were not set on fire*). To emphasize the point, they also brought in a live sheep and gave it a crown—a pretty blatant comparison of the pageant to livestock competitions at county fairs.

Who is to say why the media focused on the non-existent bra-burning? I mean, if I were the media, I would've focused on the sheep/beauty queen comparison. That shit is clever and damn funny. Who knows, maybe they felt they could draw a strong comparison with the recent burning-of-the-draft-card and burning-of-the-flag protests. (I guess it was a good time to be a pyromaniac.) Or maybe they wanted to belittle what took place; maybe they wanted to point to those rightfully enraged women and shake their heads and sigh, "Oh, those crazy feminists."

But now you know the truth. Bras weren't burned, but there was a garbage can full of cleaning supplies and porn and a goat with a crown. And really, isn't the true version of the story so much better?[29]

(see boxed text) began working with Dr. Gregory Pincus to develop her vision for a birth control pill. When the U.S. Food and Drug Administration (FDA) approved the Pill in 1960, it was monumental. By 1963, 2.3 million American women were using it.

No longer inhibited by unwanted pregnancies, women were finally able to plan their lives and have true control of their bodies and reproductive rights. But the struggle to control our bodies didn't end there. In the early days of the Pill, there were potentially dangerous side effects, which doctors often not only dismissed, but also refused to talk about with their patients. Sexism was still alive and kicking, à la "Women aren't capable of understanding basic information about their own bodies, and any woman on the Pill must be a slut, so why even give her the time of day?"

In fact, many doctors in the 1960s downright refused to give the Pill to unmarried women. It's hard to believe that a doctor could have ever been allowed to make a decision like that for his patient, but it's true.

Over time, the Pill has become less stigmatized and more of a sign of women's strength and independence. But it's important to remember that such empowerment—which our generation tends to take for granted—really is relatively new. Female sexual empowerment isn't a given. It was fought for, and it was earned. We can't forget this, because if we do—if we become complacent about our reproductive rights—well, they might just disappear.

THE FEMININE MYSTIQUE
(OR "THE PROBLEM WITH NO NAME")
In the 1960s, most women (albeit generally white middle- and upper-class women) grew up to become housewives. The problem was, being a housewife was really, really boring for many of them. If they weren't just sitting around after having finished doing shitty stuff like cleaning the draperies, then they were taking over

their kids' art projects for school, turning what was supposed to be an animal figurine into an elaborate centerpiece perfectly suited for even the most lavish of Thanksgiving tables—all out of a deep starvation for any kind of mental stimulation. They found themselves thinking things like, *Hey, I really don't love my kids. I just resent them* while tossing back their third gin and tonic of the afternoon.

The main problem, though, was that women didn't really understand why they were so unhappy. After all, they had homes, beautiful families, husbands with good jobs, and automatic dishwashers and brand new washers and dryers. Who could ask for anything more? But then why were they popping the 1960s equivalent of Xanax and sticking their heads in ovens while their kids napped upstairs (well, maybe that was just Sylvia Plath, but she probably didn't invent the idea, mkay)? Then, in 1963, Betty Friedan (see boxed text) published *The Feminine Mystique,* which is often credited for almost singlehandedly sparking the second wave of feminism. Not only did this groundbreaking book answer that question, but it also revolutionized the way women saw themselves and their lives.

These women, Friedan reasoned, were suffering from "the problem with no name"—a problem that Friedan picked apart in the book, analyzing its sources and its effects. She pointed to advertising, which was controlled by men, yet directed at women. Since 75 percent of all consumers were female, they were the ones paying attention to ads that depicted women as happy housewives who were totally psyched to "play house" rather than actually pursue their own interests. Friedan also pointed to a chaotic post-WWII society, where men (who had suffered the traumatic effects of fighting in a war) needed their wives to be mommies more than partners. Oh, also: Friedan totally hated Sigmund Freud, and she criticized him thoroughly in the book. (Basically,

Freud was like, "Hey, let's evaluate all of humanity based only on sexuality" and actually convinced people that women had something called "penis envy." Enough said.)

Friedan also thought that a lot of women's problems lay in their education. Women weren't being pushed to pursue any kind of careers after college (if they were being encouraged to go to college at all). But it wasn't just the fault of parents or teachers: A lot of girls were saying "screw this" and dropping out to have babies, for fear if they waited too long, they'd miss their chance. Future generations of men and women were being negatively affected by "the feminine mystique" as well, Friedan noted. Bored mothers were coddling their kids to death, or passing their passive behavior on to them—which was resulting in a generation of unmotivated slackers.

Clearly, this all had to stop. Friedan urged women to forgive themselves for feeling unfulfilled—and then to do something about it. She encouraged women to find meaningful work, despite what people might say, as she felt that work was good for women personally, for their children, and for society at large. The message was provocative, and women were hungry for it.

Friedan also provided an opportunity for women to talk to *each other* about this common feeling, which many women had previously thought was something that they alone were experiencing. The knowledge that they weren't alone incited an incredible amount of strength—enough strength to launch an entire wave of feminism.

TITLE VII

Believe it or not, discrimination in the workplace technically used to be legal. Employers could legally choose to hire a man over a woman because they figured women would eventually just quit in order to settle down and have babies. They could legally choose to

GLORIA FELDT (1942–)

A passion for social justice has propelled the life and work of nationally renowned activist and author Gloria Feldt. Called "the voice of experience" by *People* magazine in 1996,[30] Feldt was a teen mother from rural Texas and grew up to serve for nine years as president and CEO of Planned Parenthood Federation of America, the nation's largest reproductive health and advocacy organization.

In May of 2011, I met with Feldt and asked her what she, as a second-wave feminist, thought were the biggest differences between the second and third waves of feminism, and she responded:

> *I think every generation has to speak for itself, and every generation has to fight its own battles. I think that the second wave did a really good job of many things—opening a lot of doors, there were a lot of really great people, a lot of firsts, a lot of pushing the envelope—but what we didn't do very well was to teach the next generation about the power of the sisterhood that got us through. . . . What I hope I'm able to do today, with the things I write and say, is just to demonstrate that there's great power in working together with your allies, and particular strength and power in working together with your sisters.*

Today Feldt teaches "Women, Power, and Leadership" at Arizona State University and serves on the board of the Women's Media Center. Her recent book, *No Excuses: 9 Ways Women Can Change How We Think about Power,* reveals why women still hold only 18 percent of top leadership roles. Her previous books include the New York Times bestseller *Send Yourself Roses* (coauthored with actress Kathleen Turner), *Behind Every Choice Is a Story,* and *The War on Choice.*

hire a white candidate over an equally qualified candidate of color due to their own prejudices. Basically, employers could discriminate against employees based on race, religion, sex, national origin, or any other identifier.

Title VII of the Civil Rights Act of 1964 changed all that. Arguably its most notable accomplishment was that it put an end to racial segregation in schools, places of work, and public facilities. However, Title VII also had major implications for the women's rights movement, as prohibitions against discrimination based on sex were also incorporated into the bill (albeit at the last minute).

Of course, flaming racists and sexists were pretty pissed that the people they hated had earned legal protection. But as is evidenced by where we are today, we managed to evolve past those people and embrace the accomplishments of Title VII as basic rights.

TITLE IX

Think of the things you love to do. Maybe, like nearly one-third of American teenage girls, you play a sport after school.[31] Good for you: High school girls who play sports are less likely to get pregnant, more likely to get good grades, and more likely to graduate than those who don't.[32] Thanks to Title IX, you *can* play sports and derive all the benefits of being on a team: friends, structure, and fitness, to name just a few.

Who do we have to thank for Title IX? Second-wave feminists. Believe it or not, we are one of the first generations of women to really have the opportunity to play sports and participate in many other activities at the high school and college levels. It's a huge part of many of our identities.

But believe it or not, Title IX isn't just about getting equal funding for our sports. In fact, sports aren't even directly mentioned in Title IX. The amendment, which was passed in 1972, is actually all about equality on every academic level. Title IX mandates that nobody can be discriminated against under any educational program or activity that receives federal financial assistance.

So join a Mathematics Appreciation Club! Join the soccer team! Thanks to second-wave feminists, you can.

EQUAL PAY ACT

Imagine working the exact same job as a male counterpart but getting paid less because, essentially, you have ovaries. You come into work and leave at exactly the same time as he does (or, maybe you even come in earlier and stay later). You do the exact same amount of work (or more). You are equally dedicated, and you take your job just as seriously as he does. But every month on pay day, you glance at his check and notice that the same number isn't printed on both—in fact, those checks are far from being identical.

This used to be a standard scenario for working women until second-wave feminists went, "*Woah*. Woah. This is bullshit," and then explained to everybody that wage disparity based on gender sucked for a ton of reasons. However, cleverly enough, they didn't just frame it on a personal level. They made the argument that equal pay would help their employers too (clever ladies).

First, they argued, low wages affected women's health, as earning less decreased women's living standards, which in turn negatively impacted their work performance at large. They also argued that low wages caused labor disputes, which burdened and complicated commerce. Employers who provided equal wages, therefore, would have a happy, healthy, productive workforce. It was a win–win situation!

The Equal Pay Act of 1963 was signed into law and effectively abolished wage disparity based on sex. Or, it abolished it on a *legal* level, at least. Women still only earn 78 cents for every dollar a man earns, even though we make up 47 percent of the labor force.[33] It's a great example of how the accomplishments of the waves before us still need our help before they are complete.

ROE V. WADE

Now, I'm going to need everybody to read this section *very carefully*. Stop stealthily watching TV out of the corner of your eye. Log out of whatever social media site you are currently on. Possibly even *turn off your cell phone*. (Just kidding, put it on silent. Who turns off their cell phone?)

I can't even count the number of girls who, upon hearing me mention *Roe v. Wade* in some context, have dealt me glassy eyes and a "What's that?" It's not even okay. But, being the patient feminist sensei that I like to think I am, I then deliver the following explanation:

In 1973, the Supreme Court ruled that first-trimester abortions were to be allowed, and that all state laws that prohibited such abortions were unconstitutional. The decision (referred to now as "Roe v. Wade") was based on a woman's right to privacy, and it detailed a woman's ability to decide, with her doctor, to choose to have an abortion in the early months of her pregnancy without any restrictions.

But here's the thing: *Roe v. Wade* did not end in 1973. The decision was not simply made, then accepted. People didn't just move on with their lives. No: *Roe v. Wade* is still incredibly relevant right here, right now, because there are still people fighting vehemently to overturn it.

As of 2011, 57 percent of politicians in the House of Representatives were opposed to healthcare reform and were anti-choice.[34] Conservative extremists want to completely eradicate a woman's right to choose.

Look. Abortion is a really complicated issue and clearly a very personal one. But consider what our country would be like if women *didn't* have the right to choose. No matter what *you* would do in the event of an unwanted pregnancy, we need to allow women to make choices for themselves. And if *Roe v. Wade* is overturned—which it *is* threatened to be, on a pretty consistent basis—we will have to surrender that right to choose for ourselves. And if we surrender that right, who knows what else will be taken away from us.

THE THIRD WAVE
(YES, FEMINISM OUTLIVED BELL-BOTTOMS)

It seems to be a popular belief that at end of the 1970s, feminists looked around, realized all of their battles had been fought and won, shrugged, and resumed their daily lives. That large crowds of marching feminists put down their Pro-Choice and Keep Abortion Legal signs and went home, patting themselves on the back. That women happily skipped off to work, where a Candy Land–like utopia of equal opportunity awaited them.

Not so much.

It's true: Second-wave feminists did a lot of the frontline fighting for us. Our grandmothers did some pretty amazing things in an amazingly short period of time. But it took winning these battles to realize that there is a gap between legal accomplishments and social change.

For example, even though it's now completely illegal to discriminate against somebody because of gender in the workplace, it still occurs with upsetting regularity. So where the second wave left off, the third wave gladly took the reins—starting off in fluorescent tights and legwarmers, then on to grungy jeans and flannels, all the way to today's phenomenon that is skinny jeans.

What's It All About?

The third wave of feminism can get pretty confusing. Words like "multiplicity" and "epistemology" get thrown around a lot, and when that happens, my eyes tend to glaze over, and I wonder what's happening on my Facebook newsfeed.

Because I care about you, dear reader, and truly believe that feminism doesn't have to be restricted to a women's studies course—where big words and discourse usually hold more weight than what goes down in the real world—I trudged through feminist texts to come back to you with the official "legit" version of what the third wave is.

It seems to boil down to this: The third wave is all about the integration and individualization of feminist ideologies into everyday life and the world around us. Like I mentioned above, legal victories can only take us so far. The battle that still remains—the battle that is arguably the most difficult—is injecting feminism into the minds of society at large. And that's essentially what third-wave feminism seeks to accomplish.

INDIVIDUALIZATION

Second-wavers often wonder why third-wavers aren't as prone to organizing huge rallies à la the 1960s civil rights movement.

Here's why. While a group mentality still does exist in third-wave feminism (we do still have events with many people; we do start campaigns for social change; and we do come together in great numbers on the Internet via blogs, Twitter, etc.), modern-day feminism is more than ever a personal effort. And besides, when the goals are more complex—involving the way we as individuals think and act—marching doesn't always do the trick.

But how does individualization work? Well, there's the whole idea of rejecting social norms. Not to get all "Free to Be You and Me" on your ass, but social norms really *are* oppressive. We're each unique/different/special, and that should be more than "okay"—it should be the preference.

The most obvious example of an oppressive societal norm is today's standards of beauty and body type. No one can deny that what women of this generation are being told they should look like is more insane than it has ever been in the history of advertising.

THE RIOT GRRRL MOVEMENT

As far as I'm concerned, one of the coolest things to come out of third-wave feminism is the riot grrrl movement. Maybe it's because I'm a total hipster indie music snob. (Hey, at least I can admit it. And I avoid fedoras at all costs, so throw me a bone.) But I think riot grrrl music is about the coolest thing since sliced bread. Especially Kathleen Hanna: lead singer of Bikini Kill and Le Tigre, partial founder of the riot grrrl movement, and my *ultimate* girl crush.

Riot grrrl—an underground feminist punk movement—started in the early 90s as a result of female musicians looking around the punk movement, seeing dumbass guys with insultingly sexist lyrics and the mindset that "girls can't play," and saying, "Fuck *that*." Riot grrrl music was not only straight-up great music, it was also political, tackling topics like rape and eating disorders.

Both the movement and the term "riot grrrl" were tied to the 'zine movement (homemade, feminist-oriented, underground magazines). The members of Bikini Kill and Bratmobile (oh hey there, Kathleen Hanna) put out 'zines that filled in the gaps the music couldn't cover. There was also the element of reclaiming derogatory terms (which were often hurled at female musicians when they played in the boys' club that was the punk scene in the '90s). A fine example of this is the iconic image of Kathleen Hanna with the word SLUT scrawled on her stomach.[35]

Even the supermodels themselves are not good enough for the ads—no, they need all kinds of Photoshop wizardry and nips-and-tucks to exterminate every "flaw" and "imperfection." If we buy into this garbage (and unfortunately, many do), we're setting ourselves up for hell on earth.

Individualization comes in when you, an individual woman, accept who you are. You let the feminist value of self-acceptance work its magic in your own life. Maybe society has a fucked up ideal of what a woman's body looks like, but that doesn't have to be a part of *your* life. Take in feminism for yourself, and inevitably you will push it back into the world—your own personal force field of feminist activism. You know, the whole "Be the change you want to see in the world" thing. That's individualism.

INTEGRATION

In ninth grade, just as I was beginning to wear my feminist badge with pride, I was in a class that was comprised of ten boys and me. This wasn't really a problem—we all got along pretty well, despite the fact I didn't find fart jokes funny.

Anyway. Once they got wind of the fact that I was, you know, in favor of equality and basic human rights, they pounced on me like starving pumas. They recited every "woman get back in the kitchen" joke they could think of. They made baby-killer jokes— a powerful combination of ignorance with a super-complex and depressing topic.

And I just sat there. Because at fourteen I was still trying to figure out what feminism was, and what it meant to me. Defending myself—or feminism in general, to *boys* no less—was beyond my comprehension.

It took me a couple of years, but eventually, I figured out that I am actually capable of intelligently and effectively defending myself. Now when some dumbass tells me to make him a sandwich, the next five minutes (or however long it takes for him to run away) are his own personal hell. And it turns out that it's not the complete turnoff I assumed it would be. A lot of people *respect* me for standing up for my beliefs and myself (as they damn well should).

This kind of self-defense is living up to the third-wave standards of integrating feminism into one's daily life.

Another way to integrate feminism is in consumer choices.

REBECCA WALKER (1969–)

The daughter of second-wave feminist Alice Walker (see boxed text) and civil rights lawyer Mel Leventhal, Rebecca Walker is one of the most notable leaders of the third wave.

After graduating from Yale, Walker and Amy Richards (see boxed text) cofounded the Third Wave Foundation, which aims to "support young women and transgender youth ages fifteen to thirty. Through strategic grant-making, leadership development, and philanthropic advocacy, we support groups and individuals working towards gender, racial, economic, and social justice."[36]

Being bisexual, biracial, and Jewish largely shaped Walker's identity, and much of her work addresses those aspects of her identity. After the birth of her son in 2004, she also began to explore the topic of motherhood, especially as it relates to feminism. In addition to writing for many notable publications, she has written four books, including *Black White and Jewish: Autobiography of a Shifting Self* and *Baby Love*.

Rebecca Walker's influence on the third wave is certainly indispensable, and she continues to do great work in the movement.

For example, next time you're in line at the grocery store, you could pick up that *Cosmopolitan* off the rack. You could ignore the fact that it's really just a thick collection of ads of women making "sexy eyes" even though sex is completely unrelated to the cheese grater or whatever they're trying to sell. You could ignore the fact that the "articles" are really just frenemy-like insults hissing, "YOU'RE FAT AND UGLY! READ ON TO FIND OUT HOW TO SAVE YOURSELF BY HIDING ALL OF YOUR HORRIBLE QUALITIES SO THAT YOU MIGHT TRICK MEN (BECAUSE *SHH!* LESBIANS DON'T EXIST) INTO LIKING YOU!"

Or *maybe* you could opt for a feminist magazine, like *Bust* or *Bitch*, or, even cooler, a feminist 'zine.

You don't have to donate half your paycheck to the Ms. Foundation to be a feminist. You don't have to sign every single petition ever created to make contraception more easily available. Of course, those things help—but so does bringing feminist ideology into your everyday life. Maybe that means making sure people *know* you're not okay with sexist jokes, or with saying that something's "gay" when you mean it's stupid. Or maybe it's asking your friends their opinions about the way women are portrayed in the media—rather than slamming the way the starlet of the moment looked at that movie premiere.

As it turns out, there are many ways to make a difference without marching on the Mall in DC (although that's pretty cool too).

ENDING THE VIOLENCE

The amount of violence that still occurs against women is shocking. Of course, there are a lot of reasons it persists—everything from the rigid masculinity standards that our society forces on men ("Men are strong and don't take shit from anybody, blah blah blah") to the fact that we've normalized violence (Grand Theft Auto, anyone?). Whatever the reasons, the problem is deeper than "Hitting people is wrong." For men to be able to hurt women (though it's not *just* men hurting women), misogyny has to be alive and well.

Here are some stats:

- Someone is sexually assaulted every two minutes in the United States.[37]

- One out of every six women has been the victim of attempted or completed rape. (And keep in mind that rape is known to be one of the most underreported crimes, so the statistic is almost definitely higher.)[38]

- One in five female high school students report being physically and/or sexually abused in a dating relationship.[39]

Yeah, and that's *just* scratching the surface. This shit is real, and feminists want it to end.

We have a tendency, as a culture, to blame the victims of violence. Women are largely led to believe that they deserved whatever violent acts were committed against them. The psychological effects of being in a victim-blaming culture are as obviously detrimental as they are hugely pervasive. Third-wave feminists seek to let women know that being the victim of violence is never their fault, but rather the fault of a misogynistic culture.

But ending violence against women isn't just a third-wave priority because it's inherently wrong. It's also detrimental to our progress as a gender, and it keeps us from achieving equality. Violence is another means by which men subjugate and control us, and that shit is not okay. Many people argue that violence against women needs to be an issue that men spearhead—that, considering virtually all of the people committing such violence are men, it only makes sense that they are the ones that need to end it. But until then, feminists can speak out against violence, raise awareness about it, and truly impart to women that violent men can't steal their strength—and that we can always rise above it.

SEX EDUCATION AND REPRODUCTIVE RIGHTS

Our society has some serious issues with sex. On the one hand, porn is available to anyone with Internet access; on the other hand, in many places, it's a bitch-and-a-half to get comprehensive sex education.

The following is not a joke: Instead of learning about contraception, abortion, and STDs in a factual way that actually provides information relevant to teenagers' lives, some schools get stuck with dumbass things like the Abstinence Clown. Yes— that's a real thing: A guy dressed up as a clown juggles (because what teenager isn't thoroughly entertained by *juggling*) and then tells kids that sex will ruin their dreams. Literally. And *federally subsidized* abstinence-only groups pay him.

Fabulous.

Not to mention that for those of us who *did* manage to come away with any actual information about birth control from our sex-ed classes, there are still pharmacists out there who will refuse to give us birth control, even if it's prescribed. You know, because if we're on birth control, we must be big, fat whores, and that is *offensive* to said pharmacists.

There is still an unbelievably large population of people who are just in denial about the whole sex thing. They think if young adults are not directly exposed to sex (i.e., given an abstinence-only sex education), we just won't have it. They believe that waiting until marriage to have sex is the right choice for *everybody*. They force their ideas and beliefs on us, and they harm us in the process.

Third-wave feminists are not okay with this. They believe that there's no way around the fact that women are *going* to be sexually active, even young women—who really seem to be at the heart of this debate.

Now, it's also undeniable that teenagers aren't one homogenous group. We're individuals, and therefore, our individual attitudes toward sex and sexual behavior are completely different and encompass a huge spectrum. But no, seriously, at least some of us (and it's no small population, mind you) will be sexually active, no matter what, and it only makes sense that we should be able to be responsible and healthy about our sexual choices. We deserve to be educated, and we deserve access to choices once we are educated.

Moral of the story: Some people are really, really stupid. Which is fine. *Except* for when it interferes with our right to control our bodies. Then it's time to get involved.

CAREER V. FAMILY

Now this is an issue that, as a young feminist, I've only just begun to think about. It's hard for me, at my age, to imagine the difficult position women are put in today when they feel torn between being a wife and mother, and still wanting to pursue their career ambitions. It's also hard for me to imagine what it's like, beyond that dilemma, to face a bunch of sexist shit at work.

But this issue is something that usually brings women to feminism. Once they enter the workforce, women who have always thought their gender had already achieved equality often start to feel, for the first time, how sexism still exists.

Yes, the "glass ceiling" (a term used to describe the technically invisible but still very real barrier that keeps women and minorities from rising to the tops of their professional fields, despite their qualifications) is still very much in tact. There was a lot of talk of Hillary Clinton breaking the glass ceiling with her run for presidency. And while she definitely did make some cracks, I think quite a few women working in fields besides politics would argue that the ceiling is still there, and that they have in fact encountered it.

Women *still* earn less than men: In 2009, we earned about 80 percent of what men did.[40] We are still incredibly underrepresented in leadership positions in most major fields. Women currently make up 15 percent of corporate management, 16 percent of law partners, and less than 3 percent of Fortune 500 CEOs.[41] In the House of Representatives, of 435 members, 76 are women; in the Senate, of 100 members, 17 are women.[42]

While the lack of leadership and achievement are a huge problem, a more blatant issue is the fact that women still face workplace discrimination. It can be anything from ridiculous and annoying come-ons to inappropriate touching and worse. Because sexual harassment still exists, it's clear that there are still men out there who view women as objects, and who see their presence in the workplace as a fun perk, something like target practice. And beyond that, women have the right to earn a living without having to worry about or deal with harassment.

Women of the third wave have also come to realize that the issues around being a working woman extend to their lives at home. In their fight to get women into the workplace, feminists forgot to think about and address what would happen to women's traditional roles as a result.

The fact is, even if we are working, women are *still* doing the majority of the cooking and housework. Add a baby to the mix (I hear they're kind of needy), and shit gets complicated. Plus, women often feel guilty (both self-induced and in no small part from

JENNIFER BAUMGARDNER (1970–)

In addition to coauthoring *Manifesta* with Amy Richards (see boxed text), Baumgardner is known for her book about bisexuality, *Look Both Ways*. In it, she offers a comprehensive view of her own bisexuality and explores the pressure she felt from both the straight and gay communities to choose one identity or the other. As she stated in *Curve* magazine,

> *I think [*Look Both Ways*] relates to politics and human rights in that I'm trying to erase some of the false difference between being gay or straight. Many of us, particularly perhaps women . . . have the potential to love women or men. It's not bizarre, or a reaction to trauma or some other thing that one can use to distance oneself from that potential. I think it is through empathy and facing fear that human rights is achieved.*[44]

Baumgartner has written for *Ms.* magazine, *Maxim*, *Glamour*, *The Nation*, and other publications. Along with Amy Richards, she is widely considered to be among the founding mothers of the third wave.

society) about leaving their child if they do choose to work outside of the home. Let's just say men tend to feel less guilty.

And what about that guilt? It seems like an impossible situation: Either stay at home with the baby and give up your career (not to mention thereby reinforcing stereotypes about women), or leave your child behind, pursue your career, and feel like a bad mom.

Well, despite what many people may think, feminists don't necessarily feel that it needs to be only one way or the other. Feminists believe in the right to *choose,* and that includes the *choice* to stay home and raise a child (and, let's be honest, taking care of and raising a human is probably one of the hardest jobs there is).

The bottom line is that women still earn less than men. We still face workplace discrimination and sexual harassment. This shit still happens, and most women don't realize it until they're in the thick of it, later in their lives. It would be a shame for our generation to wait until our late twenties, thirties, and even beyond to recognize that there's a problem. We need to be aware of these issues *now*. That way, we might be able to combat them.

BODY IMAGE

What could I possibly say about body image that hasn't already been hashed, rehashed, and then made into a body-image sandwich—which we don't even want to eat, because of the carbs and mayo? Perhaps this: When I blog about body image, I usually get called out for not talking about "real" feminist issues. But it is *totally* a feminist issue—and not just because I want it to be.

Girls today are told they have to fit a nearly impossible standard, and we are starving, throwing up, and exercising ourselves to death just to meet that standard. And though all of us have not fully trudged out into the hellish land of eating disorders, it is undeniably hard to find a teenage girl that doesn't feel at least pressured to look a certain way.

And this is a problem. Not only because it *sucks* to have to live with constant doubt and insecurity, but also because—and I speak from experience—it prevents us from reaching our full potential. And that is just unacceptable.

We're going to address this in more detail in Part Six, but the point is, deconstructing our largely horrible relationships with our bodies is a major part of the third wave. While it may not seem like there's a clear relationship between feminism and body image, the third wave recognizes that there is some serious sexism and misogyny in our culture that causes women to hate our bodies—and, obviously, feminism is all about eradicating misogyny.

NAOMI WOLF (1962–)

A graduate of Yale University and a Rhodes Scholar, Naomi Wolf became a leader and spokesperson for the third wave of feminism in 1991, when her book *The Beauty Myth* was published. In the book, Wolf provides a powerful argument that beauty is in fact a tool of the patriarchy used to subjugate women. An unattainable standard of beauty is set, she argues, and then women are punished (or put in their place) for not being able to achieve it. If we women ever want to ever achieve equality, she said, we need to relax our beauty standards.

Wolf has also written about abortion (she is pro-choice) and pornography (which she believes should be eliminated, because it unrealistically portrays sex and dissuades men from desiring "real" women). She also worked as a political consultant for Bill Clinton's 1996 election and Al Gore's 2000 election, advising them on how to reach female voters. She was hugely influential in the feminist world due to her revelations about the relationship between women's body image and a sexist culture.

The Beauty Myth should be required reading for all young women. Seriously, it'll totally change the way you view your body—for the better.

The third wave also recognizes that anything that holds women back—including any form of self-hatred—is detrimental to the feminist cause. Thus, improving women's body image is definitely on the third-wave agenda.

SEXUAL IDENTITY

It's no secret we live in a society that's totally conflicted about sex. It's good; it's bad. It's everywhere; it's forbidden. And this can be super confusing for teen girls who are trying to establish their sexual identities. We're stuck in a world where girls have two options:

virgin or whore. There is no in-between. That median place that some might consider, you know, healthy sexuality? That's off limits. (A case in point is the rising popularity of "purity balls"; see the boxed text in Part Six for more on that icky-gross-yuckiness.)

Third-wave feminists think that enough is enough: It's time for women of all ages to be able to have a healthy relationship with sex. They believe we need to be open about it. We need to be able to have real discussions about it, and we shouldn't be afraid to ask for what we want. But most importantly, we shouldn't have to worry about feeling shame—whether that's because we think we're sleeping with too many people or because we're sleeping with none at all.

Third-wave feminists envision a world in which we can make informed and healthy choices about our sex lives; a world where different attitudes about sex are as natural as the desire to have it. But more than anything else, third-wave feminists envision a world where we can accept and embrace our own sexual desires, needs, and attitudes—and don't question or judge anybody else's.

AND IN CLOSING

It can be disturbingly difficult to find examples of badass women throughout the years, let me tell you. Let's just say that the women you've read about in these pages were far and above the exceptions. Centuries of oppression have made it pretty difficult for women to make their marks on the pages of history with the same frequency as their male counterparts.

But let's just take a moment to stop and think of what those pages might have looked like had equality not been such a recent phenomenon. To envision what our world would look like today if equality had always been around. Take a moment to think of the art and music that might have been created. Imagine the wars that might not have happened, and the people who might not have suffered. Of course, we'll never know for sure what would have happened had women truly been part of the picture. Not to mention that there's very little we can do about the past (until that commercialized time machine *finally* comes on the market).

But here's the thing: We can do something about the future. We can recognize the strength and bravery of these women, appreciate all that they have done for us, learn from them, and put their efforts to good use by continuing their cause and making the future they dreamed of a reality.

PART TWO

PLEASE STOP CALLING ME A FEMINAZI

(OR HOUSTON, WE HAVE A PR PROBLEM)

There are five words that will inevitably annoy the hell out of most feminists. Those words go a little something like this: "I'm not a feminist, *but . . .*"

Utter these words—followed by a statement like ". . . I totally think women should get equal pay for equal work," or ". . . it's such bullshit that I have to deal with street harassment"—and, virtually without fail, self-identifying feminists will roll their eyes and write off everything you said after the first five words.

The problem is that those feminists are then writing off the fact that your statement *was* feminist. Why should people be alienated just because they don't feel comfortable using the term "feminist" to describe themselves?

It's true: Sometimes feminists are so focused on the arbitrary plan to "get people to identify as feminist" that we tend to lose sight of what the goal of the movement is.

If we enforce the label of feminism, we exclude so many people who believe in and who could help the cause. The point shouldn't be to get people to identify as feminist—it should be to get people to identify with the feminist movement. Seemingly similar goals, but in reality, they're quite different.

Our overall goals of achieving equality and making the world a better place for everybody are admittedly huge, broad, and seemingly insurmountable without the consent of everyone in this world. So let's not write people off because they, for whatever reason, can't get behind what they see as one particular narrowly defined movement.

That being said, it's still important to examine *why* girls feel like they have to deny that they are feminists, despite having beliefs that are clearly feminist. Of course, there are always going to be people who reject things just because they're assholes through and through. (I don't think it's been proven by modern science yet, but nonetheless, I am thoroughly convinced that there is in fact an "asshole gene" that some people are just born with.) But if there's a substantial group of people, beyond the dregs of society, who oppose what you believe in, it's probably a good idea to take a step back and think about why, and about what you can do to improve.

I think there are a lot of reasons teen girls don't identify as feminists (which we're about to get into), but I think all of those reasons are elements of a larger problem: We've got a public-relations issue on our hands.

Feminists have been so preoccupied with trying to make the world a better place (silly us) that we've kind of forgotten about effectively combating negative stereotypes and projecting positive images of ourselves, in the media and in the world at large.

And the thing is that while we can tell ourselves that the way other people view us doesn't matter, it really does. I'm not saying we should change what we are as a movement because some people reject it. I'm not saying we should let those negative stereotypes impact us, or that we should bend over backward to make people like us. No, I'm saying we need to better package and present who we *are* and who we have *always* been. The product is there. (Hello, worldwide equality? Who wouldn't buy that?) We just need to sell it better.

WHY SO MANY GIRLS DON'T IDENTIFY AS FEMINIST

The mind of the teenage girl is understood by few.

As for our male peers and our fathers, I think it's safe to assume they're too scared to even try. They probably think they'd be inundated with a tidal wave of TMI involving our periods and the dilemma of Brazilian versus bikini waxing. Ironically, they'd probably just encounter stress over an approaching physics final, or musings on what to do with our latest Sims family. At least that's what they'd get from me.

And while our mothers perhaps *think* they understand us, there's no way they actually could. After all, our mothers were never our age. They were born in chin-high mom jeans and with a mastery of the omniscient stare. Fact.

Hey, I admit it: There are times when I too am at a loss when it comes to the minds of my peers. Like when I walk into the school bathroom and find a girl my age huddled against the wall sobbing, and I don't know if I should suck up the pain of my full bladder and make a run for it or kneel down on a floor that hasn't been cleaned in god knows how long and try to comfort her. It's awkward for me, because crying in the school bathroom isn't something I could ever do.

But for obvious reasons, I understand the innerworkings of a teen girl's mind more than guys or moms. So I can let you in on a secret I have unearthed over the past few years: The vast majority of girls today *are* feminists. They just don't know it.

If you were to ask her if she was a feminist, I'm willing to bet that nine times out of ten, you'd get a solid "no." But if you then asked that same girl if she thought men and women should be equal, if she felt violence against women should stop, if she felt women were treated unfairly in the media and held to an unrealistic standard of beauty, she would agree emphatically, rearing to add her own thoughts on the matters.

So then why don't girls with clear feminist values adopt the feminist label?

Well, before I go into explaining that, I have to first clarify that I'm only talking about those who have actually *heard* of feminism. There are still plenty of girls out there today who have never heard the word—or if they have, it was in passing, along with other grandiose terms such as "histrionic" and "anachronistic." (Though I imagine if you asked these girls how many DUIs Snooki has, they'd giggle, roll their eyes as if to say, *Oh, that talentless, orange, ROLE MODEL OF MINE?* and proceed to relay, in point-by-point detail, her entire history of binge drinking and legal infractions.)

Sigh. Anyway.

Reason #1: "We already have equality."

One reason that feminism might not be a popular concept to so many young American women is that we live in a first-world country where girls feel that they hardly experience sexism. For my generation, the prospect of having to struggle against gender discrimination seems as laughable as our parents' attempts to text.

But actually, we do face sexism—street harassment is alive and well; some schools still sidestep Title IX by offering less funding for girls' sports; and there are still obnoxious teachers and coaches who discourage girls from taking higher-level math or science, running for a leadership position, or trying out for a sport.

These things still happen. But when they do, girls often don't recognize them as injustices.

"Why?" you might ask, wondering if there is some kind of force field of obliviousness that self-activates with the onset of female puberty. But the reason so many of us fail to recognize the sexism that surrounds us is not that we're oblivious. (At least, most of us aren't. I won't speak for that one girl we've all been in class with— you know, the one who gnaws the erasers off of her pencils and only bothers to participate in class in order to inform everybody that the answer is 42, even though you're in Spanish class. She's probably pretty oblivious.) No, most girls are blind to it because the kind of gender discrimination they're looking for would be more akin to a Clint Eastwood period piece in which women face unthinkable violence and adversity, and their serious-faced male allies pound their fists on tables while delivering totally spontaneous heart-wrenching monologues, and grab other men by their shirt collars and throw them against walls, and women gather in crowds in front of courthouses and demand justice, and everything is kind of sepia-toned.

Except real life isn't like that.

Let's take real-life's best-case scenario. (Despite my cynicism, I realize they do exist.) Let's acknowledge that actually, many students are treated equally in the school setting, regardless of gender. Girls play on sports teams; we take AP physics; guidance counselors encourage us to apply to top-tier colleges. And in most homes, our achievements are as praiseworthy as those of our brothers. We see our mothers working as high-powered doctors or lawyers, and we've watched our older sisters create startups in Silicon Valley. Some of our dads have even let their careers take a backseat to our mothers' careers. Many of us see our parents in marriages that function as successful partnerships. And now, women are surpassing men in college enrollment: There are 77 boys for every 100 girls enrolled in college.[1]

This is the world of many young women in the United States today. And so they assume, *My mom is successful in her career and isn't discriminated against at work, so that won't happen to* me. And they may be right—as long as they are girls who were born into the upper-middle and upper classes, who attend great schools, who were born with connections that will lead them to fabulous jobs and futures. But these girls are of course indulging in an elitist line of thinking. And it's probable that they even *recognize* that fact—that their reality is not the reality for every household in America, let alone in the world. Many high schools (mine included) have seriously integrated global politics into the English and history curriculums and require community service of some kind. This goes a long way toward countering the "If I don't see it, it must not exist" mentality.

But then again, just because we learn about social injustice in school doesn't mean we truly understand it. There's a difference between empirically knowing that one is privileged and knowing it from experience and integrating that self-awareness into one's daily life and attitudes. We understand social injustice the same way a white male Republican senator understands what it's like to be a woman in the situation of an unwanted pregnancy. (Read: Absolutely no real understanding whatsoever, and whatever understanding we do have is completely tinged by our own ideals and complete inexperience with the topic.)

So when totally privileged and blessed young women consider feminism for the first time, look at their lives, and conclude "We don't need feminism any more," it's most likely because they have been lucky enough not to have witnessed or faced inequality in their own lives.

That is, at least they haven't had to face it *yet*—or haven't yet realized that they *are* facing it. Because while their less-privileged counterparts were probably introduced to discrimination and

A PRIVILEGED WHITE GIRL'S CAVEAT

I am the stereotype of the feminist movement: I am a privileged white girl.

And while I'm confident that doesn't make my opinions, thoughts, or beliefs any less valid than anybody else's, it's definitely something I'm aware of, and it's definitely something that is inevitably shaping this book. I can't represent anybody else's experience but my own. And recognizing each of our individual limitations is really important, and something that we all need to do.

Granted, I don't think we should all be walking around with nametags that read something like "Hello! I am an upper-middle-class, able-bodied, cisgender, heterosexual, white, young, female, American. Pleasure to meet you!" That'd be more than a little disturbing, plus a mouthful to say.

But at the same time, it's important to recognize that each of us have a specific view and experience with the world, and that those views and experiences don't apply to anybody but us. So often we assume things about people before we know anything about them, based solely on what we see. The truth is, we have no freakin' clue what anybody else is experiencing or has experienced unless they tell us. We can only speak our own truths. And I know that sounds like it should be coming out of the mouth of an aged hippie who lives in a shack on the West Coast and weaves his own clothes out of hemp and who took too many bad trips in his heyday on the corner of Haight and Ashbury. And just typing out all of those socioeconomic identifiers a few minutes ago had me rolling my eyes a little bit. But it's so true.

That being said, I wish that I, as a privileged white girl, at least had an *idea* of what it's like to be a person of color, or a person of a different class, in our society. I wish I could at least have an idea or a point of reference as to what that experience might be like. In all honesty, I've got nothing.

→

→ I don't necessarily want to call out feminism or any-body else on this one. Of course it's not the responsibility of those people—or of the feminist institution, or even of society at large—to seek me out and educate me about what life is like for people outside my experience. That's a ridiculously privileged, self-centered, and unrealistic notion. I have a responsibility to learn about it for myself. I have a responsibility to ask people about it. I have a responsibility to read about it. I get that. And I think I have done this.

I guess I just wish it were easier to do. I guess I wish it were a more commonly done thing. I wish, for example, that the media were based less on racial ste-reotypes and more on genuine experiences of people of color. I wish my generation weren't so steeped in political correctness that we worry so much about being offensive or seen as ignorant in our quest and curiosity for this knowledge. I wish that our society weren't so segregated by race and class on the community level. I also want to know how I can be an ally—a person who supports the rights of other races and ethnicities. You'd think by now, we'd have figured some of this stuff out.

I also think white people—as the people at the top of the hierarchy—need to take more responsibility in look-ing for these answers. Just like guys need to get more involved in advocating for women, white people need to get more involved in advocating for people of color. We need to surrender some power and do whatever we can to incorporate the realities of others into the common worldview.

Bottom line: I think it's really shitty that I'm not able to do a better job of writing about this element of femi-nism better. And I don't want to cop out, but if some-body out there thinks they can do better: You should. We need it.

inequity around the time they switched to solid food, privileged young women might not bump up against those things until they are ready to begin their careers. It very often takes leaving the relatively safe and nourishing high school and college environments to see the ways in which women have yet to achieve equality.

Reason #2: "But who am I without stereotypes?"

There are plenty of girls who want/need to hang on to stereotypical gender roles. And I'm not just talking about wearing pink, talking in a ridiculously high voice, and making every statement into a question. ("I like water ballet? I think it's really fun? I'm important and smart enough to have an opinion and make a declarative statement?") I'm talking about girls who focus all their efforts (dumbing themselves down in class, laughing at guys' jokes that aren't funny, obsessing about the way they look and dress) on getting guys to tell them they're beautiful and that they will take care of them—which, they believe, means they are set for life.

Feminism encourages us to kill gender stereotypes. And for these girls, that would mean erasing everything they've been taught about the specific ways that girls and guys should act. And that is scary, especially if they're not presented with an appealing alternative model of existence. The truly sad thing about this misperception is that feminism encourages us to kill gender stereotypes *not* to eradicate what's special about us, but so that we can figure out who the heck we are as individuals, beyond stereotypes.

Sadly, many girls don't even realize that when you become a stereotype (and this is almost too obvious to spell out, but still needs to be said)—when you follow, step for step, the stereotypical, prescribed gender role laid out for you—you are not your own person. You are not special. You really are "just another girl." When you *become* your gender stereotype, you never have to question who you actually are as an individual human being. And correct me if I'm wrong, but that seems to be the loneliest experience of all.

Reason #3: "Feminists. Ew."

Let's get real here for a second: It's pretty hard to look at someone who is portrayed as completely unpleasant and off-putting and think, *YES! I want to be just like THAT!* Yeah, the negative feminist stereotype is a pretty big reason why teen girls don't identify with feminism.

Maybe feminists of yesteryear were too busy, like, I don't know, securing us the right to freakin' vote to remember to hire a team of PR gurus or image consultants for the cause. Maybe they were too busy fighting on the floor of the Senate for the Equal Rights Amendment to stop and ask how come the media was portraying them as ugly, hairy, angry battleaxes. I imagine that when they finally had enough time to stop and look around, they went, "Oh shit. Wait, I don't even look like that."

But alas, it was too late.

The media still won't give it a rest either. Media figureheads like Rush Limbaugh still offend every human with a functioning frontal lobe by spouting hateful gibberish such as, "Feminism was established to allow unattractive women easier access to the mainstream."[2]

So if it's not true, how is this shit still largely considered fact?

The answer is simple: Feminism is threatening to those in power, and those in power are shrewd enough to know how to deal with threats effectively. To keep a threatening idea from spreading, you have to make it repulsive to people. And the more threatening the idea, the more repulsive it has to become.

So that's right: There is a legitimate reason for that ugly-feminist stereotype. That stereotype means that feminism is powerful—and that those in power know it.

Still . . . that truth does very little to change the minds of girls who would prefer to *maybe not* be associated with blatant ugliness. This is where some positive examples of feminists in the media would be really helpful. This is why it would be so wonderful for all feminists—everybody from your next-door neighbor to a major celebrity—to come out as feminists, proving that feminism has nothing to do with the way you look.

But until then, the myth of the ugly, angry, battleaxe feminist lives on, and it's more repellent than industrial-strength Deet.

Reason #4: "I just want to be a normal teenager."

Okay, so maybe this is not an answer you'd *actually* hear if you surveyed hundreds of girls about why they don't want to call themselves feminist. In fact, I've never heard a teen overdramatically sob about her desire for normality outside of a '90s-era sitcom. But even if girls wouldn't actually say this, I can guarantee you that many of them are thinking it.

Somehow, teens have the mistaken idea that if you become a feminist, it takes over your life, your personality, everything. For the record: It really doesn't.

However, it is true that when you decide to go public with your feminism, *some* people like to automatically categorize you as, "[Insert Name Here], the Feminist." For them, it's your epithet, and it's all-encompassing. Who cares if you're awesome at soccer? So what if you make a kick-ass chocolate soufflé? This is the second version of the feminist stereotype—the "if she's a feminist, then she must live and breathe feminism, and everything out of her mouth must be completely representative of the entire movement" stereotype.

I'll never forget a conversation I had with a male classmate soon after I went public with my feminist identity. A liberal, open-minded guy who blatantly declared his disgust at racist and sexist jokes, he surprised me by stating—without a hint of humor or ill will—"But you don't really look or act like a feminist." When pressed as to what he meant, he elaborated, "You dress like every other girl, and, I don't know, you seem to talk about a lot of other stuff and have other interests."

I promptly slapped him in the face, shouted "YOU BAS-TARD!" and ran away crying.

Just kidding. I have absolutely no recollection of what I did after that, but I probably made a joke about it, called him an idiot, and moved on.

My point is this: Though I am a feminist—and though I have made it a large part of my life, because of my blog, and because of my general passion for it—feminism is not the one single thing that defines who I am as a person.

And that's not just true of me: There are plenty of feminists who also manage to be professionals, artists, dog lovers, Star Wars enthusiasts, karaoke stars, lumberjacks, and marathon runners. They have families. They have other interests. They're *people*.

Feminism doesn't shape every facet of your being. Though it may be hard to believe, I've had formative experiences in my life that are separate from feminism and that have shaped who I am, what I say, what I do, how I dress . . . the list goes on. Of course, feminism has shaped me and does affect the way I act and think, but the fact that I call myself a feminist does not mean that every single thing I project into the world will be tinged with feminist ideology.

And another thing: While feminism is *like* a religion in that both have ideologies and prescribed values (and, unfortunately, extremists), feminism is in fact *not* a religion. But people often think it is—and not just any old religion, but a creepy cult, one with people who never seem to blink and who dance wildly around an urn of sacrificial unicorn blood. They think it's a cult that wants to convert you, to devour your soul and turn you into a nonblinker too. For the record, feminism is not a cult. Gatherings of feminists usually happen in the form of a benefit for a nonprofit like Planned Parenthood, or the Women's Media Center—or just at a restaurant or somebody's house—and often involve food. Like cookies. Feminists enjoy cookies, just like everybody else. In fact, if you baked me some right now, I'd show you just how much feminists like cookies. I really would.

Just as somebody might identify as Jewish or Christian, that same person might also identify as a synchronized swimmer, a pool shark, a great dad, or a loyal friend. The same goes for feminists. Being a feminist doesn't mean you have to be a feminist and only a feminist. Believe it or not, you can have a feminist identity and still be yourself.

Reason #5: "What does 'feminism' even mean?"

Honestly, I think the most common reason that teenage girls don't self-identify as feminists is that—whether they admit it or not—they don't know what one is. Understandably, girls don't want to align themselves with something they don't fully comprehend.

That's reasonable. Frankly, it's comforting to me that girls won't sign up for something unless they feel they really understand it. I wouldn't want girls to sign up for feminism the way lost souls fall into aforementioned cults and other organizations that lure people in with impressive-sounding but utterly nonsensical terminology (Scientology, anyone? I mean seriously people, it was created by a *sci-fi writer*).

But the problem is exacerbated by the fact that, even if a girl does try to figure out what feminism is, the many different definitions out there are confusing as hell. It's probable that she'll immediately be turned off by some of the limiting or extremist definitions that are out there.

Here's an example. Beatrice, age fifteen, comes across the women's movement section of her history textbook. She's intrigued (who *wouldn't* be intrigued by the fascinating history of our country?!) but confused, because while she's heard the word "feminism" before, she's not really sure what it means. The first time she heard the word, it was in the context of a joke on a sitcom—as an insult, delivered by a man to his wife when she was nagging him. But she also once heard one of her friends referring to her own mother as a feminist. It didn't seem like an insult then. So confusing.

So Beatrice does what every teenager nowadays does when they need to figure out what something means. She heads to the Internet.

First, following the sage advice of English teachers past, she heads to Dictionary.com. The following entry pops up:

Fem.i.nism (noun):

1. the doctrine advocating social, political, and all other rights of women equal to those of men.

2. (sometimes initial capital letter) an organized movement for the attainment of such rights for women.

3. feminine character.[3]

Well, that's broad, vague, and mind-numbingly dull, Beatrice thinks. *I want to know what this* really *means. What do feminists do? How do people feel about them? Is this cool? Should I care?*

So she heads to the Urban Dictionary, an online slang "dictionary," the content of which is generated by any random Internet user, and which has less to do with accuracy and more to do with being as shocking and/or provocative as possible. She types in "feminism" there and finds:

Feminism:

A movement to promote women's interests at the expense of men. Despite claims by some moderate (and misled) feminists to the contrary, feminism is not a movement for the betterment of men and women. If it was, it would be called humanism. Feminists are not concerned, for example, about the fact that four times as many men commit suicide as women, or that fewer and fewer boys attend college or graduate from high school. Feminists demand that we treat men and women as exactly equal unless it suits women to differentiate between the sexes. For example, a typical feminist will see no irony in arguing on the one hand that women need ever-greater protection from domestic violence, rape, and sexual harassment, but on the other hand that women are just as good as men at fighting, construction, farming, police work, etc.[4]

Yikes, Beatrice thinks. *I generally like the male gender—when they shower and aren't using their armpits to generate farting noises. I am also uninterested in completely repelling the opposite sex. Maybe this isn't for me.*

But then, later in the day, she takes a study break to search for YouTube videos of Lady Gaga, her idol. (She even choreographed a flash mob to "Just Dance," which successfully garnered seventeen YouTube views—ten more than the number of participants in the dance! Success!) And in her search, she comes across an interview for SHOWstudio in which The Haüs of Gaga Herself mentions feminism. Says Gaga,

I am a feminist. I reject wholeheartedly the way we are taught to perceive women. The beauty of women; how a woman should act or behave. Women are strong and fragile. Women are beautiful and ugly. We are soft-spoken and loud, all at once. There is something mind-controlling about the way we're taught to view women. . . . Perhaps we can make women's rights trendy. Strength, feminism, security, the wisdom of the woman. Let's make that trendy.[5]

Beatrice is now officially befuddled as to what feminism is. Maybe it's good; maybe it's bad. Whatever. She looks up the video for "Bad Romance" and shoves her books a little farther away.

The information may be out there, but it's just not clear. There are so many conflicting messages about feminism—it's no wonder girls have no idea what it's all about.

Reason #6:
"I'm just not into labels and group mentality."

Even if there weren't so many different definitions out there; even if we were told only good things about feminism—that it's equality, sugar, spice, and everything nice—it wouldn't fully convince us. Because we know that the world is big, and that there is always another side to the story. We were born into the age of easily available information. We're aware that almost everything we hear is biased. We're straight-up skeptical.

We're not the type of young adults who will ever sign up for a feminist-indoctrination ceremony where we sing songs about our periods, declare our undying alliance to the "sisterhood," and pass around the symbolic hammer we're going to use to smash the patriarchy.

To believe in feminism, teens of my generation have to come to it on our own.

WHY I DO IDENTIFY AS A FEMINIST

Whatever the specific reason may be, the fact is that the feminist movement has become so freakin' confusing and so far removed from both the realities and idealizations of teenage life that girls shy away from the thought of associating themselves with it. In the end, we don't want to align ourselves with something we don't understand—especially if when we begin to try to understand it, it becomes scary and alienating.

That being said, there *are* teens who have managed to foster strong feminist identities. Obviously, I'm one of them. But none of my high school friends identified as "feminist." Not one. It never bothered me, because when it came down to it, they all wrote a feminist-themed paper at some point in their high school careers; they all wrote for the FBomb; and they all defended feminist perspectives in class and life. They just weren't comfortable calling themselves feminists.

But one day, I brought it up. "Why *don't* you identify as feminist?" I asked.

They all gave their various reasons, but they can be summarized by the following: "I don't call myself a feminist because I don't consider myself part of that movement, though I do support women's rights and a feminist agenda. Plus I don't want to be segregated from other people. Calling yourself a feminist alienates people. Anyway, feminism is basically the same thing as liberalism."

Here's the thing. Like I said, I really don't give a flying fuck whether or not somebody identifies as a feminist. (Okay, maybe that's not totally accurate: I do *love* it when girls identify as feminist. It makes me warm and fuzzy inside, like a teeny tiny kitten is curling up against my heart.) Ultimately, I'm much more concerned with whether or not the people I know maintain and enforce feminist values.

I would never think less of anybody who chooses not to identify as a feminist, and I support anybody's decision to self-identify any way they want. Want to go around telling people that, while you appreciate the feminist agenda, it's more important to you to be known as a "pokemonist"? I say, "Go for it! Just don't vote for political candidates who want to restrict what I can do with my vagina! Thanks, and good luck trying to catch 'em all!"

But I will say this. There is a distinct difference between those who call themselves feminists and those who don't—and I don't just mean the willingness to take on a label. I mean the difference between being passive and being active.

Those who don't identify as feminists can claim to support the feminist cause in every way but name. When you ask them about feminism, the response usually goes something like, "Of course, if somebody did or said anything sexist, I'd do something about it," or "Of course, if it came down to a vote, I'd vote with the feminist agenda." But they're not willing to put themselves on the front line. They're not going to go out there and speak out against sexist language and actions before they happen. They're not going to go out there and advocate for the proposition that would make the vote a reality.

But when you actually identify as a feminist—as in slapping the label on your forehead—it forces you to act. As a self-proclaimed feminist, you can't be passive about your thoughts and ideals: You're committed to them, because you've told people you're a feminist, and so they will hold you to them. I don't mean they'll hold a gun to your head and say, "But you're a feminist! You have to sign this pro-choice petition!" Rather, when other people know, it activates your sense of integrity. You know you must act on what is right. Or, maybe you're not affected by peer pressure—it's enough that *you* know. You act because you're a *feminist,* damn it.

That willingness to take action is what it comes down to for me, if for no other reason than life is short. It's so fucking short. (Like, I feel like I was in kindergarten proudly drawing my mom a rainbow not five minutes ago, and yet somehow now I'm in college. How the hell did that happen? Give me my crayons back, damn it!)

In all seriousness, though. We have this one, glimmering, beautiful shot to be alive on this crazy-ass planet. I really don't want to spend my time fucking around. Yes, I want to have fun, I want to laugh, and I want to love. But I don't want to be on my deathbed and realize I really only gave it a half-assed shot. I want to be *all in,* and I want to completely and fully support everything

I believe in, and do what's right. And maybe—just maybe—that complete self-abandon to my beliefs and values will actually make a difference.

And *that*, my friend—that, more than anything else—is why I identify as a feminist, loud and proud.

DEFINING "FEMINISM" (OR MISSION IMPOSSIBLE)

Some people say that the main failure of the feminist movement is that none of us can agree on what the hell we're talking about on the most basic level. There isn't one definitive definition. We may all call ourselves feminists, but when asked, we all define the word differently.

And it's true. There is no way around it. Feminists as a group are divided, and that's confusing the shit out of everybody.

But seriously, what can you expect? Feminism is a movement that aims to unite and empower a *massive* population (who in reality have little in common aside from gender) under an incredibly loosely defined and widely varying set of goals and values. That is an incredibly complicated thing to do.

And one could argue that it doesn't matter anyway. Maybe the fact that we're not unanimous about the definition is not a totally bad thing. A word doesn't have to have one meaning and one meaning alone. I'm not even saying that the social-justice movement of feminism *should* have a single mission. Having an outline of clear rules and a few leaders with a united vision would be closer to a dictatorship, and therefore completely antithetical to the goals of the feminist movement. It's a *positive* thing that we're able to individualize such a broad movement, and that we're able to incorporate such an array of perspectives and opinions about where the movement should go.

Another argument is that we do, in a way, have a united mission. There is one element *all* feminists can agree on: equality. At a

DEFINING FEMINISM: BABES WHO SAID IT BEST

Feminism isn't just about equal rights for women. Feminism is a critical project. It looks at all aspects of life to identify those elements that might be oppressive and suggests alternatives . . . feminism, in other words, follows the critical project with action to bring about social change.
—Sally J. Scholz, in *Feminism: A Beginner's Guide*[6]

I would still go along with the dictionary definition of [feminism as] "someone—who can be a woman or a man—who believes in the full social, economic, political equality of women and men." To say [that I am a] "radical feminist" is only a way of indicating that I believe the sexual caste system is a root of race and class and other divisions.
—Gloria Steinem, in a 1995 interview with Feminist.com founder Marianne Schnall[7]

"Feminism" is not a dirty word. It does not mean you hate men, it does not mean you hate girls that have nice legs and a tan, and it does not mean you are a "bitch" or "dyke," it means you believe in equality.
—musician Kate Nash, on her blog[8]

Take Back the Night walk, if you were to go up and tap one of the marching women on the shoulder and ask her to define feminism, I'd be willing to bet you that the word "equal" would in some form be recited. (And the words "empowered," and "strength," would probably come right after it.)

So that's great. At least we can agree on "equality."

But is that enough? Because what does equality even mean? And isn't the equality that American feminists are looking for different from the equality that Congolese women hope for as they band together to get the firewood that keeps them alive, praying with every step that they won't experience rape as a war crime—an occurrence so frequent that being "ruined" is essentially a female rite of passage? And does equality even begin to hint at the complexities that arise when you try to examine the intersections between race, class, ability, religion, sexual orientation, etc. with gender? Does it even begin to encompass the true vision feminists have for the future of our society? *Especially* when there are so many different types of feminists who are all working toward related yet unique goals?

Yeah, the word "equality" is nice. But to use it to sum up what feminism strives for is just . . . puny. Though it may not be inaccurate, it is definitely inadequate.

A NEW DEFINITION: FEMINISM FOR THE FBOMB GENERATION

Here's the thing. Young women are truly sickened by the world we've inherited. Humankind hasn't learned from genocides past, and thousands of people around the world die daily because of hate. We were born into a sort of apocalyptic frenzy. We learned, from an early age, that our environment is in crisis; that our problems are global, as are our interactions. Having mastered the computer keyboard only a few years after learning the alphabet, we are connected to the world in a way our parents never even dreamed of.

Our lives are globalized, and thus so is the way we view feminism. Nuclear war, environmental degradation, infanticide, genital mutilation, child labor, microfinancing—we care about these issues. Because the unique thing about my generation is that we're more involved with community service—spanning from local to

TYPES OF FEMINISM, DECODED

In case you didn't know already, feminism is super complicated. But it actually doesn't have to be. There are a lot of things we can all agree on (like the essential belief in equality, for instance), and if we just boiled it down, the movement might be a heck of a lot more efficient (hence, I'm writing this book).

But the thing about feminism is that it's always been super vast and super divided. There's so much infighting—between generations of feminists, between feminist men and women, between types of feminists, and more.

For real, we need to stop fighting.

But until that day comes, here's a handy-dandy guide so you at least know *who* you're fighting with. (I know. So helpful.) There are probably more subtypes of the broader feminist movement than the ones listed here, but these are the biggies.

Liberal Feminism

This is kind of a riff on the third wave, in that it doesn't focus so much on change at a societal or systemic level, but more on an individual level, at which women take advantage of the opportunities offered to them. It's that one woman working her way through business school and eventually becoming a CEO, not a group of women in business suits charging through the halls of a major company, demanding a quota for women in high-ranking positions.

Socialist/Marxist Feminism

As opposed to liberal feminism, the individual doesn't matter in Socialist/Marxist feminism, which is all about the big picture. The whole system (read: capitalism) needs to be replaced. Also, Socialist/Marxist feminists believe that women need to stop watching *Baby Einstein* with their young'uns and start making some cold, hard cash, because as long as women are financially dependent on men, they're just plain screwed.

Radical Feminism

Proponents of this type of feminism would be totally into a mass charge of the women around the world waving pitchforks and torches at the evil patriarchy demanding widespread change and equality. Metaphorically, of course. Essentially, radical feminism boils down to this: "Down with the patriarchy. RAWR!" Also, some radical feminists believe in "separatist feminism," meaning they believe men and women should maintain separate institutions and relationships. Because I guess living together in harmony is an impossible goal.

Ecofeminism

Proponents of ecofeminism are also advocates for the environmental movement—which is super awesome: We should probably stop brutally asphyxiating the only habitat our species can survive in. In terms of feminism, ecofeminists believe there is a direct connection between the domination and abuse of the earth and the domination and abuse of women. Ecofeminists also draw a connection between the pollution and abuse of the earth and the *effect* it has on women. This connection is an important one, and it is one that is often overlooked in mainstream culture. Most people don't realize that women are substantially more impoverished than their male counterparts. In fact, of the world's 1.3 billion impoverished people, 70 percent are women.[9] As impoverished people, women are the most likely to be impacted by the effects of things like global warming, and they are the least likely to be able to defend themselves. Women are the most directly affected by environmental devastation, ecofeminists believe, and they have a serious problem with it. That shit's legit.

Womanism

Coined by second-wave feminist Alice Walker (see boxed text in Part One), "womanism" is also known as "black feminism" and is the response to feminism's general

→ marginalization of black women. Womanism looks at how race and class intersect with mainstream feminist ideology, but it also differs from feminism in several significant ways: 1) It acknowledges that black women in America are victimized racially, sexually, and economically and recognizes that this was not accurately or effectively addressed in either the feminist movement or the black liberation movement. 2) It actively welcomes both men and women. 3) It examines how black women's relationships with black men are different from those of their white counterparts, and seeks to fully understand that dynamic. 4) It examines and praises black women's sexual behavior and power while also recognizing their intrinsic history of sexual violence.

Womanism is obviously complex and is a varying personal experience for all who identify with the movement. But the strong common threads are its very valid claim that feminism falls short for many women of color and its main purpose, which is to provide support for their agenda of empowerment.

global levels—than any other generation has ever been. We're not just worried about white American women. We want everyone to achieve equality—not only on the level of gender, but also on all socioeconomic levels. We want to take part in saving this messy world. It's our passion and our duty.

The women's movement has achieved enormous success on the political and economic battlefields. That's not to say that there aren't battles of this kind still to be fought—because there certainly are. But given these accomplishments, the women's movement has been able to evolve into a cultural one. Today, our battles revolve around social behavior, relationships, and the media.

We are a generation that cares greatly about the world around us, but we've grown up in a society that has transitioned from the cultural influences of Virginia Woolf's writing and Frida Kahlo's paintings to Lindsay Lohan's partying and Taylor Swift's love life. It's impossible to avoid being aware of the meaningless activities of the always young and beautiful, sometimes talented. And though we do have an appetite for social justice, we consume this celebrity culture with unparalleled voraciousness. PerezHilton.com—a blog devoted to hour-by-hour updates of celebrity culture—was the fourth-most visited website by college-aged girls in 2008, right behind Facebook, YouTube, and Google.[10] These priorities are not only unhealthy for young women, but they also are virtually inescapable.

While the media and extremist conservatives (I'm looking at you, Phyllis Schlafly) would have you believe feminists want to make everybody's lives harder and want to "shove their liberal agenda down the world's throat," my generation's brand of feminism does not promote one single agenda to be applied to everybody. Feminism is as much an individual pursuit as it is a national and global effort. It's the ability to live your life to the fullest, no matter who you are. Whether that means that a young woman from Greenwich, Connecticut should earn as much as a male counterpart who went to the same boarding school and top-tier college and who has a nearly identical resume, or that a young bride in Africa does not have to suffer from genital mutilation, the feminism of our generation is about the pursuit of the life you want to live, and the creation of a reality in which that goal is possible for everybody.

The FBomb seeks to define "feminism"—while still understanding that it is a broad concept that means different things to different people. Ultimately, the members of the FBomb generation see feminism as something that has become more about acceptance and equality in all planes of life—not necessarily restricted just to legal rights, or even just to women. We define "feminism" as the pursuit of "being able to live your life in the way that supports all of your human rights and makes you the happiest, no matter who you are."

And perhaps, that's why the term "feminism" is problematic.

ARGUMENTS FOR RENAMING THE MOVEMENT

All this talk about whether we need to label ourselves as feminists in order to be one is pretty interesting, considering feminism is a movement that is generally antilabel. I mean this in the sense that feminists tend not to like it (and rightfully so) when people label certain girls as "sluts" or call any guy who wears skinny jeans and takes more than five seconds to look presentable in the morning "gay."

It's just kind of ironic that a movement that rejects labels has had such issues with its own label—especially our desire for more people to adopt *our* label. But unfortunately, the problem is even more complex than that. Yes, it's time to seriously address the fact that "feminism"—the name of the movement itself—is undeniably problematic and possibly even counterproductive. And it's time to seriously consider what, if anything, we should do about it.

Abandoning the name of a movement is nothing to scoff at. It may be "just a word," but language matters. A rose by any other name may smell as sweet, but then again, if we called roses something like "leprous fen-sucked bush-warts," then receiving a bouquet of them on Valentine's Day would probably be a far less pleasant experience. And besides, whenever "leprous fen-sucked bush-warts" were mentioned in an otherwise pleasant conversation, one might not envision the beautiful feat of nature that roses truly are.

Such is the case with the word "feminism." Why should a word that has become riddled with horrible connotations represent a movement that in reality is a beautiful thing?

If you've gotten this far in the book, you know I care about history. The history of feminism is incredibly important. However, it's also important to further this movement and its goals, and it's become more than clear that the word "feminism" is holding us back to some extent. Despite the fact that the word is loaded with history and significance and real-world suffering and glory, there are some decent arguments for changing it. They go something like this.

Reason #1: It'd be great to drop all that baggage.

While we may moan when the media plies the word "feminism" with offensive stereotypical connotations, we mustn't forget that there are some nasty connotations to the word that are in fact very true.

Feminism's history isn't all sunshine and rainbows. The movement has a legitimate history of racism and elitism. That part just doesn't get mentioned that much. Here are two reasons I've noticed.

1. When we fall in love with feminism, we not only want to, but also actively try to, ignore everything bad about it. It's a common consequence of falling in love with anyone or anything. *Feminism made me a stronger more confident person, so it couldn't have possibly marginalized other people,* we justify. Oh, but it did. Let's not delude ourselves. That's not good for any healthy relationship.

2. Our dirty past is not exactly a selling point. When trying to explain why one is a feminist, or why somebody else should be a feminist, it's probably not wise to close with, "Oh yeah, and many of the founding mothers of the movement were kind of racist, and most of the entire second wave was made up of middle- to upper-class white women." That's just not a good sell. But it's the truth.

Now, I don't want to give you the wrong idea. Feminism is an awesome, inclusive, fabulous movement, especially so by the time the third wave hit, and afterward, for the most part. The first and second waves, however, have some explaining to do.

So again, the argument for this reason is: Associating ourselves with the earlier stages of the movement (and, as a consequence, with their faults, which we do not share or represent) is detrimental.

Reason #2:
The "fem" thing kind of excludes half the world.

I've got to be honest: I understand why men shy away from feminism.

There are the masculinity standards, which, of course, would be compromised should a guy admit he supports women in any way. You know, "Any guy who actually supports women must be gay—or at the

FEMINISM AND RACE: PAST AND PRESENT

Feminism has a nasty past with race. The movement has been historically concerned with and led by white women—specifically, white middle- and upper-class women.

In the first wave, the suffragists were almost entirely white, and despite the fact that the suffrage movement was almost perfectly synchronized with the abolitionist movement, black women were almost entirely unrepresented and were rarely heard from. All too often, black women were shunned from the movement, for fear they would confuse or threaten the cause. And that was incredibly messed up, because black women had the shittiest plight of all.

During the second wave, the feminist movement was once again synchronized with a movement for racial equality, with leaders such as Dr. Martin Luther King, Jr. and Malcolm X making their marks on the country. And though the feminist movement was not actively discriminating against black women, it was not thinking about them too much. The book *The Feminine Mystique*—the impetus for the second wave—focused only on the plight of white, educated, middle-class, stay-at-home moms who were bored and depressed because they were essentially doing nothing with their lives. It's not surprising that black women—who didn't have the luxury of boredom—felt excluded, marginalized, and unrepresented by the movement.

Things are getting better. More feminist

very least a weakling—for letting the womenfolk overpower him. Real, big, strong, hetero men only like and support men." (Wait, what?)

Not to mention the "entitlement" messages our patriarchal society has been sending guys, assuring them of the power they've inherently earned because of their gender. I know plenty of guys have been brainwashed by that.

organizations are actively trying to represent a wide array of leaders and are elevating the voices of women of color. But here's the thing about "actively" trying to achieve diversity. That diversity can sometimes sway a little bit toward pseudodiversity. By pseudodiversity, I mean diversity for diversity's sake—like, at a feminist conference, offering a panel spot to a black woman just because she's black—and with the assumption that she will be able to represent "the black perspective." When put like that, the stupidity is pretty apparent, but it still happens all the time. Many feminist blogs have their "black contributor" or their "latina contributor" or whatever (even if they're not specifically called that, like *The Daily Show*'s Senior Asian Correspondent or Senior Black Correspondent . . . though that's a farce, so I think it's okay).

To me, pseudodiversity is a great indicator of the complexity of race dynamics, and how far we still have to go before we achieve true racial equality. Even within a movement as progressive and open-minded as feminism, we still don't actually view everybody as completely equal—even if we do everything in our power to advocate for that reality. I think equality means looking at somebody and seeing a person: a single body that has a unique brain and an experience that's different from *every* other body on the planet. When we try to include people of other races for the sake of their race, we're not considering what they—as a *person,* as that single body— can bring to the table. And that's an epic fail.

And please, let's not forget the boner-killer stereotypes of feminists, which also never include men.

But I'm not even talking about that. I'm talking about the word. FEM-inism.

Why would a guy—unless he was well versed in feminist theory and had been well exposed to the concept—even believe it was something he *could* be part of? After all, unless you know better, the word "feminism" might as well be a No Boys Allowed sign.

Now, there are feminists who like it that way. There are feminists out there who believe that feminism is a woman's fight, and that part of the empowerment so intrinsic to feminism means taking men out of the picture. *We don't need their help,* they apparently think. *They're the ones who got us into this shitty mess in the first place.*

And on some level, I get that argument. I do believe that female empowerment, on individual and group levels, is an important part of being a feminist. There's something amazing about being part of a group of women who are challenging and undermining the very society that tells them they are inferior. And to ignore the role men have played in our subjugation would just be ignorant.

That said, I believe that any Us v. Them mentality is ultimately unhealthy and detrimental. While there have been—and god knows, still are—misogynistic men out there who would certainly like to retain their privileged roles and opportunities, there are honestly plenty (maybe even the majority) of guys who totally believe in equality. And to block them out of our fight is only going to piss them off and confirm all the negative stereotypes about our movement. ("Man haters," anyone?)

The truth is, feminism can actually help guys too. While feminism works to eradicate gender stereotypes ("weak," "submissive") that box girls in, it also seeks to end destructive male stereotypes (like the whole "not having feelings" thing).

Beyond actually benefiting men, though, including men in feminism would only help the cause. Men deserve the right to fight with us to end oppressive stereotypes, and they deserve to benefit from it too.

Reason #3: New times call for new names.

As I so painstakingly—with love in my heart and sweat pouring from my brow—outlined in Part One, there have been three successive and seriously distinct mini-movements (the "waves"). Susan B. Anthony was a BAMF; Gloria Steinem worked a Bunny suit for social justice; and Kathleen Hanna rocked out in Bikini Kill. All three are feminists, and all three have fought for the greater feminist cause. And yet they are three seriously different people who thrived during incredibly different time periods. Not to mention that their modes of activism were wildly different. (I don't know how Susan B. Anthony would've responded to Kathleen Hanna's lyrics. Maybe she would have been leading the mosh pit when Bikini Kill started playing "I Like Fucking" or "Suck My Left One." Tragically, we will never know.)

Feminism has radically evolved many times over since its inception in the nineteenth century. The three waves, as snapshots in time, bear almost no resemblance to each other, and I'm not just talking fashionwise. (Although, for real, petticoats to bell bottoms to flannel? Indicative of huge changes, my friends). The fight began with women just wanting the essentials—the minimum that would allow them to be full human beings. It progressed into incorporating those rights into our legal system, and for society to truly get the memo that women are people too. And it has morphed into an attempt to allow our legal equality to translate to our social reality. Three *totally* different fights, when you really think about it—they're just joined under the same broad label.

And that's just looking at the progression of American feminism.

Of course, I don't want to minimize the importance of these waves, or insinuate that anything that came after suffrage or the '70s wasn't legitimately feminism. The kickass change they incited was essential. It's just that, as I look at the feminist movement now—the movement that our generation is about to inherit—it becomes apparent that this is clearly not the movement feminism started with.

So should this current movement keep the same name? Shouldn't it have a name that reflects what we are doing, right now, on the frontlines for equality? While we may appreciate the past, the fact is, that's not where we're living.

Reason #4:
"Feminism" may not be accurate anymore.

When I insist to people that I am in fact fighting for equality for *both* sexes, they sometimes snort, "Well, if you're fighting for *all* humans, why isn't it called 'humanism'?"

Since I'm primed with snark the way Alaskan car engines are primed with antifreeze, my instinct is to cast the Imperius Curse and force them to do the cotton-eyed joe . . . *forever.* And then I remember the owl carrying my Hogwarts acceptance letter was tragically sucked into a wind turbine (there are downsides even to the greenest of alternative energy sources), and I'm stuck as a muggle forever.

But I have to admit that this response—which is almost always intended to shut my self-righteous ass up—has always rung true for me.

The term "humanist" has been thrown around a lot as an alternative to "feminist." Except for that weird philosophical crap during the Italian Renaissance (which was, like, soooo long ago), it's free from historical connotations, which means we pretty much have a clean slate for defining the term. It's a word that is *totally* inclusive, so we won't get derailed by that line of argument. "Humanism" has a lot of upsides.

Another viable option is "intersectionalism." Now, even though my spellcheck angrily underscores the word in red, and even though its overly academic ring summons to mind a bunch of Ivy Leaguers wearing horn-rimmed glasses, there's a lot to be said for the term.

Because feminism is no longer *just* about gender. It truly is a movement that studies the way that race, class, age, ability, gender, sexuality, etc. intersect. Thus, "intersectionalism" wins the prize for accuracy.

THAT BEING SAID . . .
(IN WHICH I TOTALLY CONTRADICT MYSELF)

There are also some seriously strong arguments for keeping the term "feminism." And let's be honest: "Feminism" deserves to be defended.

If I were to suggest a personification of the word, I'd say this: Feminism is that crazy aunt your uptight mom begrudgingly invites to Thanksgiving and watches like a hawk, convinced she's going to slip you weed at some point. She did some seriously awesome shit in the '70s and has a lot of great stories but is still totally with it and can rattle off some great rants about Kim Kardashian and John Boehner that are surprisingly equal in the fury they impart. And really, we owe it to that crazy aunt to defend her—partially because we love her and she's awesome, but mostly because she freakin' earned it by now.

In a lot of ways, identifying as humanists or intersectionalists or whatever is a complete and total copout. It's like if some kid named Dorcas is teased mercilessly for having a silly name, and that's all people ever see her as—"the girl with the weird name"—despite the fact that she's brilliant, impassioned, hilarious, and kind. So then she changes her name to Jane. (By the way, I apologize to anybody reading this whose name is Jane or Dorcas. If it's any consolation, you rock, because, well, you're reading this book.) Would Jane still be the same awesome girl she was when she was called Dorcas? Absolutely. But inevitably, she would lose the strength that comes with being teased, the uniqueness that comes with having an odd name, and the character boost that comes with saying "fuck it" and moving on.

See what I'm saying? No? Neither do I half the time. Let's try again.

A major reason people shy away from feminism or try to uphold its negative connotations is that movements are usually associated with their radicals. This is why so many (ignorant) people think all Muslims are terrorists, when in reality, Islam is an incredibly peaceful religion when it's not perverted by insane extremists. Same goes for feminists.

I will be the first to admit there are some batshit-crazy feminists out there. There are women who, in the name of feminism, say we should create completely matriarchal societies and eschew men. They analyze the shit out of everything from a feminist perspective—whether it's a painting in an art exhibit (fair, although annoying if done persistently) or your choice to wear tight, short skirts (not cool, leave me the hell alone). They refuse to use gendered pronouns. They can't take a joke to save their lives.

I don't associate with this kind of feminism, which is, as I see it, extremist. And neither do most feminists. But this is the example that is held up, because our opponents are desperate to prove that "their" way is better. And so unfortunately, this is what some people associate feminism with.

But should we really rebrand ourselves completely just because some people are hung up on extremist stereotypes?

It matters what other people think of a movement. It really does. You're not going to be able to make a real difference if people think you're insane and just want you to shut up. And maybe they're assholes for thinking that. But at some point, you have to admit, if it's the reality, it needs to be dealt with.

Think about it: Completely overhauling feminism's public image would take a ton of time and energy—time and energy we could instead use to make our world a place of equality. I think changing the name of our entire movement is that point of bending over backward for others. I think it's the point that crosses a line.

Also . . . it's kind of awesome that feminism is vilified.

I know what you're thinking: *You think it's* awesome *that when I tell people I'm a feminist, they expect me to grow fangs and tear their limbs off?! I don't. Go to the corner, Julie.*

Hear me out though.

Question: Why do people vilify others?

Answer: When they're afraid of them and the power they wield.

It's undeniable that the feminist movement has power. Beyond the obvious (such as the cold, hard, historical facts about the change we've been able to incite), we know we have power because of the way our opponents desperately rely on stereotypes and petty insults to try to diminish that power. If the notion of "feminism" is so threatening, why would we give that power up?

I don't know about you, but I fucking *love* being powerful. And if that means I have to hold on to this frustrating, inadequate, alienating, misunderstood word, then by George I will. Because the bottom line is this: When you *feel* powerful, who the hell cares if some pathetic people don't understand the word that gives you that power? You *do,* and that power is yours.

PART THREE

FEMINISTS WITHOUT BORDERS:

WHY US V. THEM
IS SELF-DEFEATING

I t's true that the word "feminism" can be kind of alienating. But the word is just a signifier for a fundamentally important movement. The historical events, the women who made it happen, the books that promote it—they're just the shell. If feminism were an M&M (and really, everything should be more like M&Ms), these factors would be the candy coating to the chocolate that is feminism itself. Feminism has been, is, and will always be really powerful. And the movement itself—the sentiments that drive it, the truth it exposes—will always overcome the shitstorm that seems to surround it at every turn.

I find it mildly hilarious that some people think that feminism is "dead," because feminists are some of the most alive people, in every sense of the word. And of course they are. Here's the thing about feminism: Once you believe in it, once you see the truth and validity of it in every single freakin' facet of your life, you feel like you've had a revelation. It feels like you've come a little closer to all of those big questions humanity has been grappling with. You feel like you better understand everything that's happening around you—and everything that you feel and do. And if you can't feel passionate about that, then you should probably take a guided tour of Hades and consider buying a two-bedroom, two-bath condominium with a scenic view of the river Styx.

The only problem is that once you become a feminist, once you have this revelation, you might end up feeling conflicted. And that's because it's kind of alienating. It can feel like being on the outside looking in. It can feel like you've seen the real state of the world, and realized that it's downright repulsive. You feel like you're on the side of Good and everybody else, by default, is fraternizing with the Bad.

That's the thing I dislike most about feminism.

I've always understood that seeing the world in black and white, good and bad, doesn't benefit anybody. It's how wars thrive, genocides occur, and discrimination persists. It's how people who could've learned from each other, and almost certainly could've found commonality, refuse to see anything but difference—and they live a life that's that much duller for it.

We need to get rid of the polarization that defines every aspect of our society. We need to think about embracing the antithesis of what we would normally believe. We have to compromise and see the benefits in the ways others think. None of us would have to give anything up. We'd only learn and grow.

Now I can see how some of you might be thinking I've got my Julie's-trying-to-think-philosophically-but-actually-just-sounds-high hat on. So let me explain.

Feminism is for everybody, regardless of gender, race, religion, or sexual orientation (or really, anything else). Feminism as a movement is becoming less focused on equality of the genders and more about intersectionality (how gender, race, religion, sexual orientation, age, ethnicity, and socioeconomic class intersect). And it's about achieving equality on all of these levels. However, I would venture to say that gender is still the central focus point (we've got roots, baby), and that thinking about gender (specifically, how to include men) is the next big thing feminism has to take on. So gender—and bringing men into our folds—is what I'm going to focus on in this chapter.

Men can and should be feminists. But in order for that to happen, we, as a mostly (let's get real, almost entirely) female-driven movement, need to appreciate the fact that men are different from, but not better than, women. We need to respect these differences and figure out how we can learn and benefit from each other.

We need to adopt qualities that were previously characterized as masculine (whether that initial characterization was right or not—hint, it wasn't), like strong leadership skills and the ability to harness our own power. And men also need to be given a chance to develop qualities that have traditionally been cast as feminine. We need to talk about the violence and objectification that are born from trying to achieve a masculine ideal. We have to let men know it's okay to feel, and that love and empathy and kindness are not feminine, but rather *human* qualities. Ultimately, we need to reimagine a new definition of gender equality that isn't moored on either side. We need to let every individual be defined by their humanity rather than their gender.

I think feminism comes down to a single truth. We need to get rid of the polarization that defines every aspect of our society—the good and bad, the black and white—and embrace the fact that all aspects of human life and reality exist on a spectrum.

So without further ado, let's dive into this.

MEN AND FEMINISM: WHY THEY NEED EACH OTHER

Being a guy today sucks. Whether they're trying to live up to their gender stereotype (which leaves little room for weakness and denies

INTERSECTIONALITY

The true beauty of the current feminist movement is that it has progressed beyond just focusing on gender equality. It has very much become a study of intersectionality: the way multiple social identifiers factor into oppression. Kimberlé Crenshaw—law professor, writer, and thinker—is credited with first highlighting this sociological theory, and I think it's pretty effin' brilliant.

According to intersectionality, nothing's black and white. There's not just discrimination caused by racism, or discrimination caused by sexism. Crenshaw's theory points out eight main social identifiers that intersect when it comes to discrimination: gender, race, religion, ability, sexual orientation, age, ethnicity, and socioeconomic class. All of these things are interrelated factors when it comes to being oppressed and discriminated against. They cannot easily be separated from one another. It doesn't take a lot of thinking to figure out how much sense this makes.

I know that there are feminists out there who love combing through everything other feminists write with

some of the basic aspects of being human) or trying to make sense of the world without much in the way of constructive role models, it seems that guys have a lot of shit they have to deal with.

You probably weren't expecting a book written by a young feminist to sympathize so much with men, right? After all, I'm just trying to form a huge, destructive army of angry young women.

I'm just kidding. About the army thing. (I don't have the militaristic skills required to build an army, let alone the patience or attention span.) But not about how vital men are to our movement. I am very serious about that.

The truth is that feminists (myself included) spend a lot of time tirelessly working to make this world a better place for girls the finest-tooth comb available to point out what's missing—specifically, which identifiers were missed—and then accuse the author of discrimination. *Sigh.* So I'm just going to beat them to the punch and admit that I do not discuss most of these identifiers in detail in this section. I wish I could have. But there are so many things happening in the world, so many lives being lived with different obstacles and adversity, it's impossible (for me, at least) to look at it all at once. Besides, that's not how these problems need to be tackled. As feminists, we can't carry the weight of the entire world on our shoulders.

But we all need to be aware, because with awareness comes understanding, and with understanding comes acceptance. We need to take it upon ourselves to learn more about these issues, and to play our parts in trying to end discrimination based on these factors. This is why I want you to know about intersectionalism, and why I want to encourage you to learn more about it, think more about it, and try to take it into consideration as you move through the world. Only by acknowledging such discrimination can we hope to end it.

and women. And in looking at the statistics, it's clear that girls and women seriously need this help. For example, nine out of every ten rape victims are female, and one out of every six American women will have been the victim of an attempted or completed rape in her lifetime.[1]

It makes sense that women are standing up for each other. It makes sense that we're calling and writing letters to our senators, that we're gathering in the streets for Slut Walks, defending our rights to dress any way we damn well please without being sexually assaulted or attacked for it. It makes sense that we, rather than those who are more often than not the ones perpetuating the adversity we face, are supporting each other.

But it doesn't make sense for men to be excluded from feminism. Why? Because men need feminism as much as women do. And feminism needs men too.

Why Men Need Feminism

It's true: There *is* such a thing as a male feminist. And I don't mean the guys who enroll in your Women's Studies 101 class thinking that sitting in a room full of girls, calling themselves a feminist, and saying things like, "Yes. Equality. I like that thing," will get them some ass. There are guys out there who are enlightened to the plight of women in this world. They get it; they don't like it; and they actually want to do something about it.

But if I had to guess I'd say that about 98.47 percent of guys would not self-identify as feminist. Which is seriously a shame, because they really need feminism.

Let me be absolutely crystal clear here: It's not that we womenfolk need big, strong men to step in and take over because we're too weak and dainty to fight the patriarchy alone. Hell, no. It would actually be impossible to find a group of feminists sitting around discussing what's missing from the feminist cause nodding in agreement when one says, "More penises. *That's* the answer." No. Men need feminism in their lives for their *own* benefit.

I think what it comes down to is that our culture today—the same culture that feminists take issue with—is trying to dehumanize us. And I mean all of us. We all face dehumanization and oppressive stereotypes. Feminism tries to fight this and aims to make all of us able to actualize all aspects of our human (regardless of gender) potential.

So yes, men need feminism. And here are a few reasons why.

* * *

REASON #1: GUYS HAVE TO DEAL WITH UNREALISTIC BODY IMAGES TOO.

It's no secret that most women (and by "most" I mean "all, minus a few incredibly confident or lucky ones") have some issues with their bodies. But here's the thing. It's not just debilitating to girls. Guys are also suffering from body-image problems.

Statistically, the rates for guys suffering from actual eating disorders aren't anywhere near the rates for girls. But body image is still a serious problem for guys. Guys and girls both measure their worth in terms of what they look like.

Let's look at the industry of male modeling. The ugly world of beauty (the tagline for nearly every *Dateline* or *60 Minutes* special on the topic ever, I swear to god) is one we're well acquainted with as far as female models go, but what about male models? The truth is that male models put themselves through hell to maintain their physiques the same way female models do. Take top male model Daniel Martin, who has appeared on the cover of *Men's Health* magazine more than any other male model. In order to achieve those glistening, defined abs, Martin restricts his fluid intake to the level of medical dehydration. For the two days before the photo shoot—after hours upon hours put into circuit training, running, and lifting for weeks beforehand—Martin eschews the training for booze, which helps speed dehydration, which in turn makes his body appear tight-skinned, with visible veins. Also, after weeks of eating little more than pure protein and vegetables, in the last two days before a shoot, he eats an abundance of carb-heavy foods, as it pumps glycogen into his muscles, making them appear bigger. He shows up to the shoot dizzy, dazed, and dehydrated almost to the point of being incoherent. And this is the norm. He has achieved a body-type that is as unattainable as his female counterparts' twenty-two-inch waists and pin-thin legs. (It's also important to note that in high fashion, men aren't escaping the "dangerously skinny" thing either: Twenty-seven-inch waists and androgyny are rapidly becoming the preference.[2])

And while it's reasonable to question whether models (who make up a minute percentage of humanity) are really representative of the whole, it all has to start somewhere. The same evolution that occurred for girls is starting to happen for guys. True, images in the media aren't the only things that contribute to unhealthy body standards, but they do matter. It's a giant, blinking, Las Vegas Strip–style sign that guys are on the same fucked-up track we are. And they're having about as much fun trying to be Taylor Lautner or the Bounty paper-towel guy as we are trying to be Gisele Bündchen.

To make matters worse, guys aren't event allowed to cry, or even bitch about how messed up and impossible it is. They're not allowed to dump a container of hot fudge into a pint of Ben & Jerry's Phish Food and go at it (I've obviously never done this). They aren't allowed to react to this bullshit in any way, shape, or form—which is awesome, because, as we all know, bottling up your emotions is *really* healthy.

REASON #2: GUYS SUFFER FROM OPPRESSIVE GENDER ROLES TOO.

Guys are supposed to be rocks, inside and out. They are supposed to be defined more by their muscles and brute force than by any complex or unique personality trait. Ideally, they should physically be so steely and impervious that they could plausibly be cast in a Transformers film . . . as an actual alien Transformer. If we were to look inside these ideal men, we'd find a tangled mess of barbed wire encapsulating a ravenous lion decapitating a tiny bunny. There would probably be a camouflage color scheme thrown in there too. Guys *certainly* aren't allowed to let the world see that they do in fact have emotions. No, they throw those feelings to the feral beast within.

But here's the problem: Guys *do* have emotions. Guys live an external reality that is in complete contradiction with their internal reality. So what can guys do when they experience real honest-to-god feelings? Well, for those who try to adhere to these masculinity standards to their utmost ability, they have to disconnect. They must detach themselves from their emotions. And it's not just emotions like "sad" or "ecstatic." It's emotions like "empathy" and "sympathy," which, when you think about it, is pretty damn scary. So guys can either detach and live a life numb to a true range of human emotion, or live in a state of contradiction. Not the greatest options.

The woes of men don't end there. Oh no. On top of embodying various types of metals inside and out, guys must also be "success-ful." But the definition of male success is quite elusive. It doesn't necessarily mean having a great, loving family and friends who care about you. It's probably not about becoming an abstract painter, or being the type of passionate, energetic high school teacher who inspires a group of jaded and self-defeating inner-city kids to want more for themselves via the power of the pen and self-expression. No. In order to be successful, guys must be cunning. They must get ahead of others in order to obtain success, which is usually defined by two things: money and power. In fact, though I kind of hate to use the word "winning" (Charlie Sheen connotations abound), it has become kind of synonymous with "masculinity."

Men feel as much competition and pressure as women do. They have to be strong. They must conceal their emotions. They need to obtain wealth and power. But while we ladies generally deal with this pressure internally, forcing ourselves to get excellent grades and taking out our issues on our bodies, guys are far more external in their expression of the same pressures and competition.

Why do guys like violent video games so much? Why do they feel the need to physically fight (or at least threaten to), even over the stupidest stuff, in a way girls rarely do? Why do they put younger guys through ridiculous hazing, which ranges from the gross and uncomfortable (I've heard of senior athletes forcing underclassmen players to eat ten Big Macs in less than ten minutes) to the seriously violent and dangerous (being beaten with two-by-fours)? Better yet, why do they subject themselves to such degrading abuse at all?

Guys engage in violent activities (whether simulated or real) as a way to release the pressure, but also, circuitously, as a way to prove their masculinity—as a way to make that competition with other guys an actuality. Guys strictly monitor each other to sniff out and point out "weaknesses" in other guys, which gives them some illusion of feeling stronger and more masculine.

I've always suspected that's why guys love telling jokes about women and gay guys. Even if a guy swears up and down he's not sexist or homophobic, by telling these jokes he is, at the very least, reminding the world he's a straight dude—clearly not the alternatives, which he so disdains.

And what about guys who dare to take on qualities that could be considered feminine? Like, for instance, guys who care about their appearance, who wear tight clothes, or who are just generally considered "effeminate"? Well, those men are threats. For guys clinging to masculinity standards for dear life, who use those guidelines as a complete roadmap for how to exist in the world, they're terrifying. For some guys, it's a seriously deep terror rooted in the threat of losing their own identity. They see other guys rejecting what has been prescribed of them based on their gender, and they're terrified of the consequences of doing the same. Because if they were to really examine themselves, if they were to reject the masculinity standards that shape their entire identity and personality, then they might just find that they never actually had an identity to begin with. And really, what's scarier than that?

But forget the implications for jerks who give any guy who refuses to live up to masculinity standards a hard time. Let's consider how this actually affects the guys who reject traditional masculinity standards. Specifically, let's consider gay men. I asked a young gay friend of mine about his experience, and he had some pretty eloquent things to say.

"Being a gay man has instilled a sense of displacement, no matter where I may be, or who I'm with," he said. As a man, he explained, he feels the pressure to meet masculinity standards—which he (and other gay men) may manifest by engaging in and promoting promiscuity. But he also feels a kinship with women, as he understands what it's like to be marginalized. "Being a gay man [means] trying to overcome both male and female stigmas," he said. "Gay men and feminists have similar ambitions, but it's hard, because gay men are ultimately men, so they have to strive to promote a sense of masculinity that works for them *and* goes hand-in-hand with the feminist doctrine of personal pride and worth."

And that's how a gay man feels in the context of an overall peaceful and unbothered state. That's not even considering what happens when bullying, violent hate crimes, and homophobia at large get thrown into the mix.

In this society, adhering to the standards imposed by masculinity means never developing your true identity, never taking the opportunity to find out who you really are. Expressing feelings and exploring interests—including things that aren't strictly "manly"—are part of being human. But if you want to be the stereotypical man, you have to forget about those things. Just like we girls have to forget about enjoying food and having interests outside of shopping and boys.

Sometimes when I look around and see all of my peers, guys and girls alike, desperately trying to live up to their prescribed gender roles, often at the expense of their own well-being, I feel like I'm crazy. I wonder, *Am I the only one who didn't get the memo? Should I be more preoccupied with how many calories are in my food than the fact that it's buttery and delicious and my stomach is so happy it's as if there is a wild conga line proceeding through it? Should I be spending more time trying to get a boyfriend? Is that what life is all about?*

And I'm sure there are guys who wonder these things too. Who look around and see how they're expected to put as many hours into ESPN and the weight room as they do into basic functions like sleeping and eating, all so that they can talk the talk and walk the walk. *Is this really it?* they must think. *Is this all we're supposed to care about? Things like sex, sports, and food? Of all the things available to us in this world, even if those things are great, are these the* only *things we're able to come away with?*

We're not crazy, those of us who see through all of this bullshit. We're just living in a society that's trying—and largely succeeding—to box us in.

So yes, it sucks when guys do box womenfolk in. It sucks when they force us into paradigms like "bitch or pushover" and "virgin or whore" and "bitch or bro." And they need to be held accountable for that. They need to be shown the error of their ways, and they need to stop. But before they're ever going to be able to stop, they need to be released from their own boxes.

We all need to escape being boxed in. We all need to realize what's being done to us, and we need something to guide us through to a better place. Something like—oh, I know!—feminism.

Finneus and Bartleby Join the Lacrosse Team

To better illustrate my point that oppressive male stereotypes result in misery and violence, I'd like to tell you a little story about my two favorite imaginary teenage boys, Finneus and Bartleby.

It's freshman year. The first semester goes by pretty uneventfully. Other than a brief flirtation with the chess club (Finneus has a slight crush on Hester, the chess club president—and, I mean, who wouldn't?), the two didn't really get involved in any

THE MAN UP CAMPAIGN

Girls and women can yell and scream about the violence that's being committed against us. We can raise awareness, petition, and take self-defense classes. And we do. But I think we can all agree that in order for real, systemic change to occur, we need to end the problem where it starts. We need to involve men in the campaign to end violence.

The Man Up Campaign—cofounded by Jimmie Briggs and Karen Robinson Cloete—works to do just that. The Man Up Campaign was created to "give young people a voice in developing models of change . . . in order to break the cycle of trauma and misinformation unabated [that] violence against women and girls bestows on individuals, families, communities, and societies around the world."[3]

Through pop culture, the arts, sports, and other things that are actually relevant to the lives of the youths they work with, the Man Up Campaign educates, fosters leadership, and creates a community among kids in order to work toward a less-violent future. Find out more at www.manupcampaign.org.

activities. They're confident that by the time they apply to college, Xbox and PSP gaming will be considered a legitimate extracurricular activity, not only because of the required dexterity and coordination, but also because of the true commitment and dedication one needs to be able to stay in the exact same position on a couch for hours on end.

But by second semester, both boys are starting to wish they had more of a social life. They watch enviously as senior boys stroll down the halls, girls' hands in theirs, talking about last weekend's awesome party, made even more awesome by the fact that ever since Dan's mom became semidependent on Vicodin, she's totally down with them drinking in the house. Finneus and Bartleby start to worry that if they're not like those guys—the lacrosse bros—then maybe they're just nerds. Maybe the school doesn't see them as the awesome World of Warcraft masters they really are. Maybe they're seen as pussies. And that is unacceptable.

Thus they hatch a plan. They both sign up for lacrosse try-outs, and by a stroke of sheer luck (and a rampant case of food poisoning caused by the lunch lady's eczema making direct contact with the mac and cheese, which wiped out most other prospective players but which both boys happened to avoid), they both make the team. After a few practices, they even start to get pretty decent, and things are looking up. Instead of completely ignoring him, as she used to, Hester now rolls her eyes in disgust at Finneus as he strides down the hall using the standard-issue lax walk—a cross between a drunk chicken with a limp and a young Ray Charles. Bartleby even starts dating this girl Taryn, who has a slight proclivity for devil worship, but other than that, she is *totally* cool. All seems well—at least, until the fateful weekend before The Big Game.

All of the freshman lacrosse recruits are invited to a senior boy's house. They swagger in, ready to get their underage drink on—and, more important, to be ushered into an age-old tradition of sports-induced brotherhood. Instead, they are ushered into the basement, where hell begins. The seniors douse the new recruits in ice water and turn fans on them full blast. They force the boys to start moving, yelling out, "Jumping jacks!" and "Sit-ups!" If anybody fails to comply, they get punched in the stomach.

Bartleby wants to cry but quickly sucks it up. He looks over to get a glimpse of Finneus, to see if he's scared out of his mind too. For a split second, he sees Finneus's profile. It's completely stoic and intense, making Bartleby feel even worse: *What kind of man am I if I want to cry because of jumping jacks?* He quickly turns away, but not before a senior notices him looking around.

"You either do what everybody else does, or you're out!" the senior screams. "And if you're out, we're going to make your life a living hell!"

Bartleby says nothing. He complies.

The seniors then line up shots of booze and make the freshmen down them. They keep refilling the glasses. Bartleby feels like he's going to throw up. But he looks around and sees all the other boys dutifully tossing back the alcohol. These will be his brothers. This is what men do. If he survives this, he'll belong. The rest of the night is a blur.

A few days later—at Taryn's insistence that something is wrong—Bartleby tells her what happened. She starts to cry and insists that they tell somebody, which just pisses Bartleby off. Doesn't she get it? If he tells, it means he can't deal. Being a man means doing whatever it takes to win the respect of your fellow man. If he tells, it means he fails the test, even after going through all that hell in the basement that night. And the truth is, he'd rather be dead than go through the rest of high school being known as a pussy, and the rest of his life remembering the shame of his failure.

That's how he realizes that it would have been easier if he didn't talk to Taryn about this at all. That's how he realizes it's easier not to talk about his feelings, not to deal with the hard emotional stuff. And, come senior year, that's how he's able to do the exact same thing to the incoming freshmen boys.

Why Feminism Needs Men

So climbing onboard the SS *Equality* will help men. But it will also undoubtedly benefit the movement as a whole.

Feminists have been talking for a long time about the need for a change in our ranks, and it's true: In order for feminism to be successful as a movement—in order for us to really get shit done

FROM THE MOUTHS OF ~~BABES~~ DUDES

I firmly believe that a government of the people, by the people, and for the people should take an interest in those people and their well-being. I believe that the rights to life, liberty, and the pursuit of happiness are significantly infringed upon without access to healthcare. I believe that everyone is created equally, and should share equal rights before the law with everyone else, and that the most basic expression of this equality is in the freedom to love and marry whomever one chooses. I believe that the government should not interject itself into the most private of individual places by trying to exert control over a woman's reproductive choices. I believe that workers have the right to organize and bargain for benefits, wages, and consideration. Furthermore, I believe it is the government's duty to protect these rights and public interests from the influence of individual and private interests.

I am defending women. Not because they asked me to do it, or because they need me to do it, but because its the right thing to do. I am defending

on a widespread scale, with change that actually improves our lives socially, economically, and politically—we need to involve men.

Here's why.

REASON #1: WE NEED TO GET STUFF DONE *NOW.*

Here's the thing. The patriarchy still exists. And it's fucking powerful.

Of course, our goal is to get that shit dismantled, but that's a huge goal. Our global society is structured entirely by this patriarchy, and to completely eradicate it without the help of *lots* more people would not only be incredibly difficult but would also inevitably take a lot of time.

And we don't have time. We can't wait a couple of decades to

> women because they are human beings who are enti-
> tled to the dignity and consideration of that condition
> like anyone else. How can we say that we aspire to
> the virtue of our ideals, like equality, when we enter-
> tain positions that denigrate our wives, girlfriends,
> sisters, and mothers? I understand it's popular in
> culture to see women as objects of our lust who have
> silly and emotional ideas and mannerisms, but is that
> the world we want to leave our daughters (when we
> have them)?
>
> Besides, whenever I don't know how to feel about
> a specific issue and am looking for a little moral direc-
> tion I look to Pat Robertson. We all know how Pat
> Robertson feels about feminism. [He said,] "Femi-
> nism is a socialist, antifamily, political movement that
> encourages women to leave their husbands, kill their
> children, practice witchcraft, destroy capitalism, and
> become lesbians."
>
> I look to Pat Robertson and do and feel the oppo-
> site of what he's instructing.
> —blogger Eitheror of The Daily Kos[4]

get rid of violence against women. We can't wait for decades for equal pay for equal work. We need to take care of this stuff now.

I'm not saying we should "give in" to the patriarchy. I'm just saying there's a way for us to more effectively work within the confines of it while still attempting to enlighten the world to move past patriarchy.

It's already annoying enough to think that women are *half* of the world's population, yet we're still somehow seen as an unimportant minority that doesn't really have a say. For example, consider politics, a realm in which women are still definitely a minority. In the United States, women hold only 17 percent of the seats in Congress and are only 24 percent of state legislators. And yet, in the 2008 election, women constituted 54 percent of voters.[5]

So though half the country is female, and though we are in fact the majority of voters, the gender make-up of our country's political institutions hardly reflect this fact.

But if men—who do make up the majority in government, not to mention every other important institution—supported us and allied with us, fighting with us on our behalf as well as their own, how could we possibly be denied (she asks, possibly naively and definitely optimistically)? As great as talk of revolution is, as awesome as it would be to band together against sexism and the patriarchy and just completely reject it, if we realistically want to get shit done, we need to work within the system—at least *until* we eventually reach a point of equal representation in realms such as politics. And who better to help us do that than the guys who run it?

Besides, if half the world's population (men) don't feel attached to this movement in any way—or worse, if they feel excluded by it—then they're going to resist it. They're going to rebel against the thing that they perceive as not wanting them to thrive. It's no different from women rebelling against the patriarchy. We need this to be a movement *everybody* fights for—a movement everybody wants to be part of.

REASON #2:
PEACE AND NONVIOLENCE DEPEND ON IT.

Imagine a world in which violence wouldn't occur with anywhere near the frequency that it currently does. A world in which violence is not tolerated, but more important, in which the reasons for its occurrences are addressed and eradicated.

Imagine a world in which men would no longer be afraid to express their feelings, their fears, and their insecurities instead of bottling them up; in which they wouldn't think that hitting and hurting were their only options.

Imagine a world in which men wouldn't feel threatened by

some perceived diminishment of their all-important masculinity, and wouldn't therefore feel the need to assert control at all times.

Wouldn't we all be better off?

Of course we would.

The patriarchy's very existence depends on the oppressive social construct of "masculinity." Domestic violence and violence against women, hazing, wars, sexism, imperialism—all of these things are a direct result of the social construct of "masculinity" and the pressures it involves.

If more men incorporated the ideals of feminism into their lives, they would be able to see these external pressures and express their feelings instead of tucking them away in some unexplored corner of themselves for all of eternity. There would be far less violence in the world, because many of its causes, like the unrealistic masculinity standards men desperately try to live up to, would no longer exist.

REASON #3:
EQUALITY SHOULD BE ALL-INCLUSIVE.

It's plain hypocritical to preach equality of the sexes when in reality you're only looking out for one sex. If you're going to fight for equality, you can't promote one sex as flawless and the other as the purveyor of all things evil. You can't expect or want women to ever have *more* power than men. If you do these things, then you are, in fact, sexist. It might be going too far to say that excluding men from the feminist movement is the same as promoting sexism, but I certainly think the current way we're approaching equality and attempting to achieve it is a wee bit skewed.

So, let's get real. Feminism needs men, and men need feminism. And to all who disagree—to all the women who believe this is "our" fight and that men are the enemy—I ask you this: How has that been working out for you lately?

GENDER BLENDING: WHY ENDING THE MALE/ FEMALE DICHOTOMY IS KEY

We've become so certain that genders are polarized—that there are men and women, that they must act certain ways, and that that's it.

Maybe that's why we're still so transphobic. When people identify as transgender—as in having a gender identity different from their assigned sex—people get freaked out, because it totally threatens their ideas of what "female" and "male" really mean. If gender weren't so polarized—weren't so boxed up and neatly wrapped into these narrow definitions—we would just be able to accept that gender identity is a spectrum. In order to create a world that is rooted in equality, that is more accepting of everybody, we need to figure out and get comfortable with that difference.

I'm not trying to make the case that we should do away with gender altogether, but people seem to forget that gender is not synonymous with sex. Gender does not accurately describe who we are biologically, but rather portrays everything else that makes us men and women. Gender can, and should, be fluid. The complete polarization of gender—in addition to being oppressive—is not a reflection of reality. Real people aren't strictly feminine or masculine, nor should they be. Restricting people to one inherited set of characteristics is a poor way to run the world. There are traditionally feminine qualities that are really valuable to society, and there are traditionally masculine qualities that are really valuable too. We serve humanity best when each of us embodies all of those valuable qualities.

As long as gender remains polarized, women will never enjoy anything but a false kind of equality. Because that's the kind of equality we have now: fake.

Think about it. It seems to me that equality has become about women imitating men, and ultimately acting in a way that allows them to be accepted into the ideal of masculinity and male power.

FROM THE MOUTHS OF ~~BABES~~ DUDES

I think the greatest challenge facing feminism is that a lot of feminists don't realize that they are feminists. In the zeitgeist, in American pop culture, there's this idea that a feminist is someone who wants to take away men's rights, which is ridiculous. I'll never forget this: my U.S. history teacher asked my class, when I was a senior in high school, "Who among you would identify as a feminist?" One person raised his hand. It wasn't me; it was the kid in the classroom who was ridiculously far-left. Mention Ronald Reagan and this guy would start sneezing or something. But not a single other person in the room did. Clearly everyone supported equality of the sexes and equal rights, but still, in 2010, that misconception was out there. And it still is. But the demonization of feminism continues to be probably the biggest problem facing feminism today. The ideas are sound and people have accepted them, but the identity is in jeopardy. Do I consider myself a feminist? Unequivocally.[6]
—Zach Wahls, twenty-year-old LGBTQ rights advocate

We're "allowed" to play on the same field as men, but we still have to play according to the same rules—rules that were designed by and for men. Essentially, a woman is equal to a man when she has been deemed able to keep up with him—or, in few circumstances, actually match him.

Now, I have limited experience in corporate America (except for my brief stint as the acting CEO of Pepsi. Just kidding. Or am I?). But I'm going to use the inner workings of the American workplace as an example anyway. I've heard that many women come to feminism after having entered the workforce, and after considering what I have to say here, I think you'll see why.

It may seem like women have achieved "equality" just by being in the office at all, and it's true that having some of the same high-powered jobs as our male counterparts is a huge and relatively recent victory. But when we get the positions we're after, we may not be equal at all. And if we are, it's because we're conforming to the standards guys have set for themselves. It's because guys were so kind enough to *let* us into their world. And even then, we're still forced into the unrealistic dichotomy of "pushover or bitch," so that guys can still exert some semblance of control over us, even when we've achieved "equality."

Conforming to men's definition of success is not equality. Playing by their rules, imitating their strategies of getting ahead, being satisfied because we're now *allowed* to be there is not equality. You don't see CEOs looking at traditionally feminine qualities and valuing them enough to incorporate them into their own approach to leading a company. You don't see very many big businesses giving their male employees benefits like paid paternity leave (hell, a lot of workplaces still don't offer paid *maternity* leave) or offering flex-hours to make work–life balance easier for working dads. *That* would be equality.

The model that men have created for running this world is imperfect. I mean, hello wars, capitalism, sexism. I'm just saying, imagine what might have happened if women had been in charge from the get-go. Maybe one lady at the round table of chief feminine goddesses (because we probably would've established a political system of collectivism rather than hierarchy) would've been like, "You know what would be cool? Let's battle another culture because we arbitrarily decide we disagree with them over something and kill a lot of innocent people who have kids at home and dreams yet to be fulfilled!" And all the other sensible ladies would've been like, "Oh! Wow! Nancy! Thanks for sharing, but maybe governmental leadership isn't for you. Have you considered channeling that anger into an athletic outlet like wrestling or extreme badminton?" Or you know, something along those lines.

Ideally, neither men alone nor women alone would be in power; rather, it would be a combination—and a balance. We need to meet in the middle and collaborate. We need to compromise over what equality truly means. Because while a lot of the fight for feminism has been the fight to have the rights that men have—the power, the economic opportunities, etc.—it wasn't to *become* them. I think we've gotten slightly confused along the way.

It seems to me that incorporating more traditionally feminine values into the way this world is run could do us all a little good. And as women, we need to have the confidence and impetus to realize that these qualities *are* valuable and *should* be implemented. We need to realize that yes, women can and should take on qualities that were once reserved for men, but men have to reciprocate. They have to start caring about their feelings. They need to start compromising too.

Equality should mean meeting in the middle, not women emulating men or forcing ourselves to take on masculine characteristics.

Men can and should become feminists. But in order to encourage that, we need to reimagine a new definition of gender equality that isn't moored on either side. We need to let every individual be defined by their humanity, not their gender.

Only once we accept this—that things have changed, that there's no logical reason to discriminate or to be afraid of others, that there's this thing called progress that the human race should rally behind, and that we're allowed to exist in a way separate from categories and stereotypes—only then can the idea of feminism being truly available and practiced by everybody be a reality. Because—oh shit!—that fluidity and acceptance is what feminism is.

PART FOUR

FEMINISM AND THE INTERNET:

THE GOOD, THE BAD, AND THE UGLY

We celebrate technological advances like they're national holidays. Or at least that's what the around-the-block lines that form in front of Apple stores every time a new iProduct is launched indicate to me. I only go into the Apple store to flirt with the guy at the genius bar who looks like a nerdy Taylor Lautner, so admittedly I'm not the authority on the subject, but it seems that this obsession with technology has permeated every aspect of our lives.

Right after I graduated high school, my school implemented a "tablet" program. Every student is now given a cross between an iPad and a regular laptop as a replacement for notebooks, textbooks, pens, and the other standard tools. The tablet is supposed to do it all: Teachers download copies of lesson plans and other resources, textbooks can be downloaded in digital format, and a virtual notebook comes standard with the device. Across the country, students are now often given these tablets as early as elementary school.

Considering that I am currently sitting here massaging a chronic back spasm caused by years of carrying around a back-pack full of ten-pound textbooks and overflowing notebooks that often makes people wonder if I am some kind of hybrid teen girl/arthritic eighty-year-old man, I clearly think this tablet thing is an amazing development.

Now of course, the tablet program isn't exactly the norm for the (far too many) grossly underfunded, overcrowded schools across the nation. Each school district has to prioritize differently, and god knows that paying teachers and the electricity bill probably ranks higher than investing in a high-tech digitized version of a paper notebook you could buy for ninety-nine cents in a drugstore.

But who knows? In a decade or two, these tablets could be standard. After all, it seems that once we implement a technological advance on any level, it's only a matter of time before it's ubiquitous—and before we can't believe how we ever accomplished anything without it.

And there's no better example of this phenomenon than my generation's relationship with the Internet. Even though human-kind up until now somehow managed without it, to us, life without the Internet seems like the plot of an apocalyptic horror movie, or even a death sentence.

But despite my generation's overwhelming Internet literacy, when I started blogging, I found myself constantly having to explain to my high school peers what I was up to. Upon hearing that I started a blog called the FBomb, many of them assumed I was cultivating a perverse, violent online community for future delinquents. And if the actual title of my blog was confusing, the concept of blogging stumped more than a few. Many still think of blogs as if it were 2001, as if they're online diaries in which people can complain about how hard life is, complete with eloquently detailed rants about how rough it is that there are only, like, four

CURRENT FEMINIST YOU NEED TO KNOW: JESSICA VALENTI

Born and raised in New York City, Ms. Valenti is probably best known for her fabulous blog community, Feministing.com, which was created in response to the underrepresentation of young women in the feminist movement. The blog is seen as extending the third-wave movement to the Internet, where much of the feminist organizing and discussion now takes place. Feministing covers feminist topics from the überpolitical to the pop culture–oriented to how feminism relates to the personal lives of the Feministing bloggers.

From Feministing, the book *Full Frontal Feminism* was born. The book is a sassy overview of why feminism *is* cool and how it directly relates to the lives of young women today. Since FFF (which is one of my favorite books—everybody should read it), Valenti has also written books about society's double standards *(He's a Stud, She's a Slut)* and America's ultimately harmful obsession with "purity" and virginity *(The Purity Myth)*.

Jessica Valenti is living proof that feminism did not die in the '70s, and that it is in fact very much alive. I'll take it even further: Valenti is living proof that it's cool to be a feminist.

different toppings available at the cafeteria's salad bar and only one variety of fat-free dressing, which just tastes like dirty gym socks.

Blogging, at least in my experience, is far from a narcissistic, self-indulgent experience. It's about forming a community of likeminded people who come together and learn from each other—and who, in the case of the FBomb, find validity in their own ideas and voices. It's an opportunity to organize and incite action. It's a source of unity.

And I'm also pretty convinced that it's the future of feminism.

THE GOOD:
WHY THE FUTURE OF FEMINISM IS ONLINE

One of the attitudes older feminists seem to have about my generation is, essentially, that we need to get our asses into gear.

After all, they petitioned door-to-door for the ERA. They held
conscious-raising sessions. Hell, they slammed their livid bodies against the doors of the Playboy Club to protest violent pornography. So when they watch us tapping away on our computers
and calling it activism, it makes sense that they'd be like, "Um,
no, I think you're confused. That's not activism, that's actually the
ancient art of sitting on your ass."

But, in defense of technology, I have to say: The Internet is one of
the greatest things ever to happen to the modern feminist movement.

Community-Building, Organizing, and Online Activism

The Internet has allowed feminists—who are an incredibly large
and diverse group of people—a place to convene. Sure, it's a virtual
convening, but we gather nonetheless.

We can unite by reading blogs, or by blogging ourselves. We
have an instantaneous way to share and encounter ideas with a
potentially vast number of people. You truly can't find the quan-
tity of receptive readers that blogs cater to in any other format.
The capability of blogs to create a constant flow of ideas (that is,
beyond the weekly or monthly limitations of print periodicals) is
also invaluable.

Blogs are also inherently democratic. Readers, in the form of
comments, arguably have as much say as the post's author does,
and often, reading the comments section of any given blog can be
just as rewarding and enriching an experience as reading a static
post. Comments sections create a fluid conversation among people
from different perspectives, backgrounds, and identities, turning

CURRENT FEMINIST YOU NEED TO KNOW: LATOYA PETERSON

A certified media junkie, Latoya Peterson provides a hip-hop feminist and antiracist view on pop culture with a special focus on video games, anime, American comics, manga, magazines, film, television, and music. She is probably most known for her work on Racialicious (a blog about the intersection of race and pop culture), although she has also contributed to feminist blog Jezebel and other outlets such as *Vibe, The American Prospect,* and *Bitch* magazine. She regularly speaks on topics of race, gender, and social media, and she is currently working on projects related to race, pop culture, and video games.

This is what she has to say about the blogosphere in relation to minorities:

> *While I am hard on the blogosphere, my work in tech has taught me that there is one huge benefit to the blogosphere—that there are just so many folks that are out and around and speaking and writing and thinking publicly, and most of us are searchable. So the whole dynamics of the blogosphere really reinforces what many of us have been saying for years and years—it isn't that we [minorities] aren't around, it's that you aren't listening.[1]*

a singular opinion into an entire debate. And that conversation is always just a link away.

This is the main way communities are built online: Readers of a common blog are actually able to carry on a conversation and form bonds. They get to know each other in a deep and real way.

Beyond the blogosphere, though, we can join feminist-oriented Facebook groups and meet other like-minded feminist souls, or organize an event and alert an entire online network to its occurrence. We can spread awareness of our cause through mass-email chains or via awesome organizations (like Change.org) that have a mission to raise awareness and gain support for worthy causes. There are plenty of sites where users can create their own petitions and otherwise be in charge of creating their own form of change. There are even websites (like Kickstarter) that allow people to raise money for their projects or ideas.

And while these websites and new opportunities for communication and connections aren't limited to the feminist community, our movement has certainly reaped their benefits.

Outreach and Awareness

Thanks to the rise of YouTube, anybody with Internet access can watch and learn from videos like the It Gets Better series,[2] and a bevy of feminist-oriented vloggers has gained thousands of faithful viewers. For example, vlogger NineteenPercent made waves with her feminist critique of Beyoncé's single "Run the World (Girls)"[3] and with her subsequent series of videos posted on Feministing, which exposed a large audience to a type of feminist thinking they might never have encountered otherwise.

And what about those girls who live in places and with people who have metaphorically cemented a wall between themselves and feminist thought? The Internet allows them a way out. A teen girl might live in a close-minded, adamantly anti-choice community, but she can always go online and find Planned Parenthood's website. Empowered with information, she can make better choices for herself. Even browsing the web for something totally unrelated to feminism (say, for example, Beyoncé's new hit single) might lead her to feminist analysis and thought. The funny thing about search engines is that even the most random search terms have the power to inadvertently expose people to new ideas—such as feminism.

Here's a real example. On the FBomb I once wrote, like,

CURRENT FEMINIST YOU NEED TO KNOW: LENA CHEN

As a sophomore at Harvard College, Lena Chen achieved e-infamy by starting the (now defunct) blog Sex and the Ivy. Her first-person accounts of sexual experiences, alienation, and the true state of undergraduate life at the world's premier academic institution spurred campus discussion, prompted media attention, and garnered a loyal following. Quickly becoming a controversial figure, she has been criticized by some as "morally reprehensible" and praised by others for encouraging frank sexual dialogue.

Lena now considers herself a "reluctant sexpert." Why so reluctant? She explains:

> *I hate that there's an entire matchmaking and self-help industry profiting off of people's insecurities, peddling antiquated romantic advice, and guaranteeing "true love" as long as one follows all the rules. There isn't a foolproof, one-size-fits-all formula when it comes to things as complicated as love and sex, so I'm the last person who's going to claim that I have all the answers. While I do stress certain basic principles (communication, safe sex, equality, to name a few), I don't purport to have the magic solution that will snag you your soulmate, nor do I even think that everyone needs a soulmate in the first place.[4]*

Lena graduated from Harvard in 2010 with a bachelor's degree in sociology and a minor in women, gender, and sexuality studies. She currently works as a blogger, writer, and media producer promoting sex education, healthy relationships, reproductive well-being, and queer rights. You can follow her online at Twitter (@lenachen) and TheChicktionary.com.

five sentences about Megan Fox while she was one of the top-ten most-searched female celebrities on Google. Literally thousands of people were directed to that FBomb post from Google. Naturally, about 95 percent of them were horny dudes looking for sexy pictures of Her Royal Hotness, but many of them (as evidenced by the comments that were left) were teen girls.

The same goes for the FBomb's weekly feature, Support Women Artists Sunday. Every Sunday we profile a badass female musician. We include a biography, a couple of music videos, and a link to that artist's iTunes page. As a result of the feature, girls have Googled their favorite artists, come across a Support Women Artists Sunday post, and visited it. Once there, they are intrigued and continue to click around, eventually finding posts about teen-feminist dilemmas, or posts with views on a recent news item that match their own. And then they stay.

Making International Feminism "Real"

The Internet also allows us to begin to bridge the gap between different global feminist movements. With the Internet, we can see what our feminist sisters in India and Saudi Arabia are up to. And then we can support them—and use their stories, perspectives, and ideas to shape our own movements.

As I explained in my introduction to this book, discovering female feticide and infanticide was what first got me involved in feminism. The fact that such atrocities could not only be committed, but also be so common, such an accepted part of other cultures—that was what lit the fire within me. But even though what I found in all my research and reading on the subjects made me irate, it was still something I only read about. It wasn't something I could see or feel. Only later, when I was connecting with actual girls abroad via the FBomb, did the adversity that women face on a global level become truly tangible.

A few months after starting the FBomb, I received an email from a fifteen-year-old girl from Jordan. She sent me a blog submission about how difficult it was to be a teen feminist in the Middle East. She wrote of how free speech and empowerment are weakened and undermined by patriarchal control and widespread rejection of anything Western. She asked that I post her submission under a pseudonym, because if anybody were to find out what she had written, she could be in great trouble.

She continued to write posts over the next year—about her feelings on the headscarf (hijab), and about honor killings, which is when (generally) the patriarch of a family kills (or directs other male relatives to kill) a female relative because she has brought dishonor to the family. So-called dishonorable activities include having an affair and, in some extreme cases, simply talking to a man to whom she is not related.

That's when I felt the connection. That's when it became real to me. Here was a girl who had witnessed things I'd only read about, and who lived in a culture that promoted values different from the ones we live with in America. She had *emailed me*. It wasn't in the printed text of an article or the spoken words of a teacher. It was a direct connection. She was real and part of *my* life now.

It was then—when I could actually point to somebody real who had witnessed these things—that I finally realized, on a deeper level, "This shit actually happens."

I know how incredibly privileged and naive that sounds. Of course I should've known that it was happening and, as a rather curious person, I *had* made an effort to understand what was happening to women around the world. But I think it's hard, when living in a culture that is so *relatively* seeped in equality, to truly comprehend what is happening to women around the world. When, as a young woman, I go to school every day with boys my age, when I play on a sports team, when I go to college, it's difficult to truly comprehend that there are women in this day and age who are not only prevented from doing all those things, but who are also brutally harmed with regularity and who are considered less than human. I don't know what that reality looks like. I have absolutely no concept of what that feels like.

CURRENT FEMINIST YOU NEED TO KNOW: COURTNEY MARTIN

Courtney Martin is a writer, teacher, and speaker living in Brooklyn, New York. She is also a total badass feminist and an idol of many (including me).

She is also the author of feminist-themed books such as *Click: When We Knew We Were Feminists* and *Do It Anyway: The New Generation of Activists.* However I (as I'm sure is the case for many others) was first introduced to Courtney's brilliant writing via her first book: *Perfect Girls, Starving Daughters: How the Quest for Perfection Is Harming Young Women.* It's a close examination of women's unhealthy relationships with their bodies, and it was nominated for the Books for a Better Life award.

I asked Courtney about her thoughts on the current state of women and body image, and why it's an important issue, and she had this to say:

I think [the issue] is both incredibly representative of the unfinished work of feminism and also this great opportunity to bring people into a feminist consciousness. There are so many messages about our bodies and about beauty, and how that translates into our worth as women and as human beings more generally. So it's like this universal and incredibly toxic issue of our time that I think is really a powerful opportunity for women to fight back—for girls and women to fight back.

Courtney continues to do great work on behalf of women, in terms of body image and beyond.

It used to be "real" to me in the way that watching a movie or reading a book feels real: plausible, but constrained to a screen, written about on a page in a book. You turn off the TV, close the book, and stress about how you really need to study for that bio quiz, or think about who you're hanging out with that night. It feels real only to a point, because that's the only way most people in first-world countries have experienced it.

Ultimately, the Internet is a tool that is beyond powerful. Just as it has changed the way business is conducted, the way we define our relationships, and the way we communicate, it has also changed the way we create, maintain, and grow social movements. I'm not saying that the Internet will solve all of the feminist movement's problems. There are still pervasive issues that have nothing to do with communication and accessibility. But at least with the Internet, we're able to remove some roadblocks in a fresh and largely effective way, and that is nothing to sneeze at.

THE BAD AND THE UGLY: THE UNFORTUNATE RISE OF CYBERASSHOLES AND THE DUCK FACE

But then again, the Internet is not all rainbows and sunshine. Despite all of the amazing advancements it has afforded us, technology has also created an effective way for us to inflict harm on ourselves and others. Its vastness and permeability are things to be lauded, sure, but they're also the same things that can shroud our generation in an uncensored and unprecedented darkness.

When Jerks Use Computers: The Proliferation of Online Harassment

I personally know a thing or two about bullying. Somebody very close to me was teased all throughout his childhood. This friend was a sensitive kid, with maturity beyond his years. His philosophical and ever-curious spirit was unappreciated by his peers, who rejoiced less in staging elaborate plays in their basements or writing short stories for fun and more in destructive and aggressive sports and roughhousing. As the seal of his death warrant, my friend was overweight and unwittingly found himself the target of cruel jokes and taunting from an early age, which hardly abated as the years passed.

The cruelty of young children is a thing as mysterious to me as it is utterly heartbreaking. Where do kids as young as six or seven learn that they should systematically destroy kids they see as different? Where do they learn that tormenting a peer will make them feel superior? How do they make other children cry and yet feel nothing—or worse, vindication?

I've heard the theories: Kids from damaged homes—kids who witness violence or who suffer from neglect—will target their peers; kids target others to distract attention from their own flaws. I've processed these analyses, and on some level, they make sense. They're probable. But I don't think it's the whole truth, and I don't think it's true for all bullies. Maybe I'll never really understand.

After months spent coaching him to walk away and to never stoop to their level, to less than positive results, my friend's mother felt that enough was enough. She stormed into the elementary school and demanded to see the principal. When he appeared, he must have sensed the fury crackling through her body, because he also summoned the guidance counselor. (He claimed it was because of the counselor's child-psychology expertise, but I'm inclined to believe he took one look at her and wanted a witness.)

"Are the children physically harming your son?" he asked her, his face carefully arranged into a veneer of concern.

"No," she responded, because nobody had in fact ever actually touched my friend. "But they torment him every day. They call him names and insult him."

The principal nodded and turned to the guidance counselor. She nodded and replied, "Well, you can't actually punish a child for saying something to another child. And besides, the boy your son says is bullying him denies he has ever said anything. So there's nothing we can do."

The bullying continued through middle school. My friend is a person with a strong character and a strong sense of justice. He never fails to make me laugh or to really make me think. I have always admired him. And I can think of nothing that ever wounded me more than the fact that he was forced to deal with people who were so weak and insecure that they felt they had to target him. Nothing makes me more livid than thinking of the teachers who just couldn't seem to do anything about it, even when a child made a comment directly in front of them, in their own class. My friend transferred to a smaller middle school by seventh grade. Enough was enough.

Words can crack a person's soul. A mere sentence can cause wounds so deep that it takes novels of words spoken by determined and pure souls, later in life, to heal them. Sometimes (more often than not, in the cases of true cruelty) those wounds turn to ugly, permanent scars. And yet my friend's mother was told nothing could be done—that punching and kicking are the only forms of bullying, and that hands and feet are the only weapons accessible to children.

This is why the Internet terrifies me. It takes a particularly cold or damaged child to say the nasty, hurtful words that were hurled at my friend. But you don't have to be quite as cold to type them. There still has to be some semblance of a hole in your heart, some chill that circulates in your blood—but it's almost too easy. Bullies are essentially cowards by nature—they are too weak to have integrity, too concerned about themselves to comprehend or care about what they do to others. And both the Internet and texting are the ideal tools for the cowardly bully.

In the past few years, this kind of story has begun to pile up in the news: Megan Meier, age thirteen, committed suicide because a boy she had connected with on MySpace began insulting her, saying that he'd heard she wasn't a good friend. Coupled with her already existing clinical depression, this proved to be just too much. In a truly disgusting and horrific turn, it was revealed that that "boy" was actually the mother of one of Megan's classmates.[5] Jamey Rodemeyer, fourteen years old, committed suicide in October of 2011 because his peers relentlessly teased him because of his sexual orientation.[6] The list goes on: Tyler Clementi.[7] Ryan Halligan.[8] Phoebe Prince.

Phoebe Prince was a fifteen-year-old Irish girl who had recently moved to Massachusetts. She was being cyberbullied by girls at her high school. (In case you're not aware, cyberbullying consists of endless torment via Internet, chat services, and texting.) Phoebe also suffered old-fashioned bullying, with classmates calling her a slut and completely defaming her character. She committed suicide.

I remember some of my friends reacting to the story in shock. "Isn't suicide a little drastic?" they whispered. "I mean, they were just text messages. Sure they were mean, but mean enough to kill yourself?"

I wasn't that shocked that Phoebe hanged herself in her closet. Saddened and deeply depressed? Yes. Absolutely. But not all that shocked. I had witnessed what cruel words, lobbed continuously—day after day, week after week, month after month—can do to somebody who's young . . . or to anybody, really. But at age ten, at twelve, at fifteen, at eighteen, you don't have the perspective or the thick skin to ignore it, and you're self-conscious enough as it is. When your entire world is school, and school is torture, and the people in it torturers, it can feel like there's nothing to live for. When you are forced into a terrified and defensive state for eight hours straight, Monday through Friday, it takes a huge emotional and physical toll on you. There's the persistent dread, every morning, of having to actually throw yourself back in to that environment. There's the despair at how many *years* of that treatment remain. There's the feeling of complete helplessness and the lost faith in humanity when your teachers turn a blind eye, and when your parents—the people who are supposed to protect you—force you to continue the same existence, day after day. There's the loneliness. The degradation. The complete lack of self-esteem and self-worth. There's the emptiness.

"Words hurt" doesn't even begin to cover it.

You can be fat. You can be a "slut." You can be gay. You can be anything that deviates from the norm, and you can—and probably will, at least at some point, to some degree—be bullied. In fact, it seems the list of identifiers that makes you a target grows infinitely, while the list (the golden, sacred list) of what makes you safe increasingly narrows. So really, it's not about being different. In fact, in this day and age, all you have to do to be bullied is to be online or own a cell phone.

Verbal bullying and abuse have been around for a long time. What hasn't always existed, though, are modes of communication that make bullying that much easier and more persistent. In a plot worthy of its own horror movie, it seems that bullying other people to the point of suicide is becoming a hobby for some teens. And considering the *Consumer Reports* finding that Facebook exposed a million teenagers to bullying and harassment in 2010, we could even consider it a widespread hobby.[9]

Online harassment is as easy as typing a few words and pressing SEND. And when they don't have to face the person they're talking to, people are more impulsive about what they say. And after they press SEND, there's no way to undo it. And now it's even possible to harass people anonymously (thanks, technology)!

I believe that bullying is a feminist issue and should be treated as such. A movement that seeks to achieve equality should, by its nature, combat any actions that promote inequality. When somebody bullies another, they are establishing a hierarchy. They are sending a message to the person they bully, and to all who witness the bullying, that they are somehow more worthy than whomever they have decided to torture. They point out that person's flaws in order to eradicate any threat to their own superiority. Feminism doesn't stand for this treatment, because it's absolutely wrong and is complete and total bullshit.

The Internet has become a platform for spreading hate. While it's easy to see the benefits that technological advances provide for the feminist cause, it's impossible to ignore the harm it has also caused. It's impossible to ignore its casualties.

I've heard the arguments that bullies have always been around and will always be around, and that technology has not necessarily increased their numbers but has just augmented their visibility. And of course, it's important to note that technology does not create monsters. Rather it's a tool used by monsters, and they, the people, are the ultimate problem. This may all be true, but it's an inadequate response.

I think I've witnessed a best-case scenario for how somebody can survive and overcome childhood bullying. My friend, the one I mentioned earlier, finally found what he loves to do and is thriving. But even though he's finally happy and successful, I can still see it in his eyes sometimes. He still has trouble fully trusting his peers. There's still a deep sadness there that I'll probably never be able to understand. Though my friend's case is one of the better outcomes a victim of bullying can hope for, it's not good enough.

Maybe the devastating suicides of those who were cyberbullied and the misery of the people who continue to be cyberbullied can be productive for society at large. Maybe—if we continue to hear these

THE HATE STOPS HERE

We Stop Hate (WSH) is a nonprofit organization dedicated to empowering teens to accept and love who they are by encouraging "teen esteem," or teen self-esteem. The organization is founded on the belief that teens who are happy with themselves won't put others down, and that together, we can stop bullying. WSH is also known for its incredible YouTube vlog channel, which enables teens from all over the world to share their own stories and to encourage their peers to stop hate.

We Stop Hate's founder, Emily-Anne Rigal, is a teen from Williamsburg, Virginia. She was inspired to create the organization because in elementary school, she was teased so relentlessly for being overweight that she decided to switch schools. Though the switch allowed her to gain self-confidence, Emily-Anne never forgot about her experience with bullying. As she put it, "At seventeen, I now know the benefits of embracing who I am, but memories are made to last—even the painful ones have a purpose. So my heart goes out to young people struggling with self-acceptance. I believe it is my life's work to help others turn self-hatred into self-love."[10]

So what's her advice for teens who have experienced or are currently experiencing bullying? "Teens who are being bullied should focus on spending their life with people who make them happy, not who they have to impress," says Emily-Anne. "In doing so, they will realize that people who put you down or make you feel bad are not important. We only live once, and the most important thing is for us to be happy. So we must all be true to who we are and make it a habit not to be critical about small things."[11]

Check out We Stop Hate online (westophate.org) and on YouTube (www.youtube.com/westophate), and join the teen-esteem movement.

stories and acknowledge their unacceptability, rather than write them off as an unchangeable reality—we'll finally *see* these bullies and the pain they cause. Maybe we'll realize that being bullied is not a "phase" that must be endured, or a part of growing up, but rather a torturous, unnecessary hell that's unequivocally wrong.

Maybe we'll actually do something about it.

All the Internet's a Stage, and We Are Merely Players

Cyberbullying is probably one of the worst things to emerge from technology, but there's another really freakin' annoying phenomenon that has emerged from our collective addiction to technology. This is the sometimes entertaining (but for all the wrong reasons) occurrence of the Internet's promotion of "performance."

Gender itself is intrinsically a performance.

Men perform their masculinity by acting tougher than they actually are. They perform on the basketball court and the football field. They perform when they are hazing their slightly younger peers.

Women perform their femininity by choosing clothes that will emphasize their reproductive abilities (I'm talking boobs and hips, people) and, more blatantly, their sex appeal, and then by manipulating their bodies to fit those clothes. They perform for guys by laughing at the right moments, by pretending they're weaker than they are, and sometimes by kissing other girls for guys' enjoyment.

And while any of these acts could be seen as a natural expression on the part of any given person, the fact that we're all doing this—that we all do this to prove something about who we are as a woman or as a man—makes it a performance. We're all essentially putting on a show, which means being disconnected from who we truly are.

Remember what I was saying in Part Three about how none of us are fully human because of the way society is today? How we're still very much trapped by our gender and kept from expressing ourselves as individual humans, rather than as just another guy or another girl? This is what I'm talking about. And the Internet has the tendency to make this about ten times worse.

My entire sixth-grade class simultaneously discovered MySpace overnight. I'm sure there are readers out there who were born into the Age of Facebook and who are therefore quite befuddled at this casual mention of another social networking site. Well, children, gather round. I shall tell you a tale of the olden days, circa 2005. Believe it or not, there was a time when MySpace was not merely a showcase of cheap "escorts" and burgeoning pop-punk-alternative bands with guyliner and flippy man-bangs galore. No, there was, in fact, a time when MySpace was the shit, and I live to tell the tale.

Like I was saying, in sixth grade, when we were all grasping for some tangible indication of our social status, MySpace seemed to emerge out of the woodwork. Finally, a way to know how popular we *really* were! We could actually *count* our friends and compare them to other people's. We could flaunt our inside jokes by writing on our friends' profiles for all to see. We could post a profile picture that captured our cuteness at its ultimate peak, and flaunt it to all! Rejoice! O, happy day!

Oh, the saga of the profile picture. We would skip lunch to take pictures of ourselves, just so that we could change our profile picture daily. I remember pictures taken in the girl's bathroom, our little preteen bodies positioned on top of toilets, blowing kisses to a friend who stood below with a camera. (Why we thought posing in a bathroom, *directly above a toilet,* was adorable is beyond me at this point, but it made sense at the time. Let's just say none of us will ever become art directors for *Nylon* magazine.)

And then there was "the duck face": The girl holds the camera above, just so, so that her head, which is tilted up, is the only thing in the frame other than a bit of cleavage (which, at twelve years old, was virtually nonexistent, but that didn't stop any of us). To perfect the duck face, you must make your eyes as big as possible. You must look like a cross between a creepy horror-movie Victorian doll that comes to life to terrorize everybody and a recently abducted victim of the zombie apocalypse. Your lips must resemble, as the name implies, a duck. You must purse them and then shove them away from your face as far as you possibly can. If you don't feel the strain in your lip muscles, you aren't pursing and shoving them out far enough. Pain is beauty. I think this is supposed to emphasize one's cheekbones, and admittedly, it does. Your cheekbones will look sharp and angular enough to slice a nice, thick block of gouda. But then again, your lips will look like you stuck a pair of wax clown lips on your face but without any intention of entertaining at a child's birthday party. I personally never understood this aesthetic trade-off, but I guess it works to attract the menz. It takes practice and dedication to hone this look, obviously. Not just *anybody* can pull off the duck face. But that didn't stop virtually every preteen in the nation from trying.

The honing of the profile picture was the first form of online performance I can remember. Some girls even became obsessive about it, choosing to spend their weekends on hours-long photo shoots.

I remember being really concerned about this phenomenon in middle school. I didn't want to spend time taking pictures of myself. I didn't want to obsess about my appearance. I was genuinely worried about the mindset my friends were starting to adopt, using their profile pictures as a lens for viewing themselves. They were thinking of those profile pictures as a true representation of who they were. It freaked me out then, but now, in retrospect, it seems so minimal—a drop in the bucket—compared to what online performance has become.

So what's really so evil about performing? After all, in 2010 Angelina Jolie made US$30 million for performing.[12] Something that could potentially give you the ability to hire an assistant for the butler for your fourth vacation home in Tuscany can't be all that bad, can it? But then again, despite what many a completely smashed dumbass desperately trying to get lucky might tell us, none of us is Angelina Jolie. And the performing we're doing is far more potentially damaging than anything Jolie could come up with (with the possible exception of knives in bed).

Performance breeds competition. Ask any young girl, and they'll tell you the same thing: Competition is an intrinsic part of girl culture. We are constantly trying to outperform each other. We're all trying to play the role of "perfect teenage girl" better than everybody else.

Who is this person, this perfect teenage girl? Well, she's beautiful (like, duh) but approachable. She's thin but not "scary" thin. She's funny but not funnier than guys, who all adore her. She doesn't let people walk all over her, but she's not strong-willed or opinionated. She's smart, but she's not a brainiac or a geek—and if she is, her other qualities (like beauty and willingness to party) must be pretty excellent to overcome that severe pitfall.

We're all competing to be a person who doesn't have deep, meaningful life experiences. We're all competing to be a person who always achieves what she has to in order to get by, but never more. We do all that we can to never have to feel the sting of failure (and therefore, never to learn from it). We all compete for boys who are generically good-looking and who do generic things (like play sports and adhere to masculinity standards), so that we never have to face the challenges (let alone rewards) of an actual partner.

Yes, the truth is, we're all competing to be the best rather unexceptional human being. Actually, we're not even competing to be her. We're competing to *play* her, to perform the role, because, really, nobody is that perfect girl. And to do so, we must hide who we actually are—if we know who we are at all. Because many of us don't even have a clue about the f'd up game we're playing. As we develop eating disorders, as we manically scheme the demise of our "competition," as we generally miss out on getting to genuinely know ourselves and other people, most of us aren't even consciously aware that what we're doing is trying to achieve a standard of perfection that looks more like mediocrity.

But the thing that's really f'd up is that now, this competition isn't confined to the seven hours a day, five days a week, four years of our lives in high school. Now—thanks to Facebook and the like—it's permeated almost every single hour of our school lives and beyond.

It's not that whenever we're not in school we're on Facebook. (Although I have met people whose main extracurricular activity is prowling their Facebook newsfeed.) It does seem, though, that every event revolves around the anticipation of being online and of digitally sharing our personal world with our network of friends. We capture every party, every girls night out, every event—notable or not—on our cameras. Do we do this to preserve memories? Maybe. But the fact that we immediately upload those photos to Facebook speaks volumes about our main motivation: to show everybody else what we've been up to.

It also leaves us absolutely no time to figure out who the hell we are, beyond this f'd up little competition of being the perfect(ly average) girl. Yes, this "game" has been around a long, long time. Girls for decades have competed for popularity, have compared themselves to other girls, and have tried to take said other girls down in order to be at the top. But at least that game was largely confined to school hours and some time on the weekends. Now—because of the Internet, social media, and the way technology has permeated every facet of our lives—it's constant. We have no time to just take a breath and step back, back into our true selves.

So the people we "play" on social networks—the constantly

uploaded photographs of us with our friends at a party or concert, the posts on our friends' walls riddled with invitations and inside jokes, the statuses that tell the stories of the lives we want—it's all a part of the big game, the never-ending competition. But the effects of this game, this constant competition, manifest in more ways than just an underdeveloped personal identity. It's mental and emotional. It's mind games. But it's also corporal.

Social networking and technology haven't just changed our normal interactions with others; they have also physically permeated our bodies. Comparing our bodies to other girls' bodies isn't exactly a new phenomenon. Walking down the hall and immediately judging other girls for how they look and then instantly comparing them to ourselves—this is the quintessential experience for teenagers and has been forever. (Research shows that the way girls feel about their bodies is strongly influenced by their friends and peers.[13] Some researchers even argue that peers influence their friends' perceptions of their own bodies more than the media.[14] So if you claim you haven't done this, you are either lying or the most secure person alive.)

We've all looked at other girls and thought, "Oh my god, her legs are so skinny." And "Why did she get blessed with genetic air brushing, and not me?" We've all stood next to girls in the bathroom and wished our stomach were as flat as theirs, our hair as shiny, our boobs as big.

But now Facebook means that we do this even more than ever before. We flip through other girls' pictures and compare our lives and our bodies to theirs. From person to person, the level on which this occurs varies, sure. There are girls who subconsciously look at pictures posted by their Facebook friends and—though they don't actually admit it to themselves—internalize the fact that they feel inferior to that image. There are also girls who are active about it, who flip through the photos of their Facebook friends, aggressively comparing themselves to each and every one, slipping into self-hatred and mentally calculating how many calories they are *not* going to consume the next day. And yet for all this comparison, it's scary how similar our pictures actually are. We exert a shit-ton of effort into presenting ourselves in the same way as others present themselves. Anyway you cut it, Facebook gives us a way to be influenced by our peers *at all times,* and our bodies and body images are suffering as a result.

Constantly performing is stressful. Combine the pressure of constant performance with the other stressors and bullshit in our lives, and it's no wonder we're totally overwhelmed, and it's no wonder we lash out—at our bodies, at our peers, at ourselves. But more than anything, this type of performance and competition encourages us to slip into stereotypes rather than developing authentic identities. And that's what I take issue with the most.

HARNESSING THE GOOD, DISCARDING THE BAD AND THE UGLY

Technology and the Internet are an intrinsic part of my generation's unifying experience. I think every single teenager I know has, at least once, heard a parent—who's sitting at a computer, randomly clicking on buttons, slapping the computer (has that *ever* helped? ever?)—angrily and dejectedly mumble, "I can't. . . . It won't. . . . Help." Or my favorite: "Help me with The Facebook. What is 'a wall,' and why am I writing on it? That seems rude."

My generation (and the one after it) is growing up in a very, very different world. And not just because toddlers now learn to read while curled up in their parents' laps with an iPad instead of tiny children's books. Technology—and especially, the Internet—has completely altered the way we think and act, and has changed the way we see the world—for better and for worse.

Because we grew up with the Internet, it's easy for young men and women of my generation to think it's a basic right. It's easy for us to forget that it's something that hasn't always existed. But in fact, the Internet is a privilege. No other generation was bred with the mindset that unlimited access to the Internet has afforded us. No other generation has had such an amazing tool—a tool that opens up a world of possibilities—at their fingertips. And we need to recognize that and remember that with privilege comes responsibility. And then we need to live up to that responsibility.

It's a mighty power we're wielding. We're seeing that right now, as protests around the world use the Internet and social networking to spread awareness, rally support, and effect real social and political change. It's an example we should follow. We should not waste this amazing tool on activities that wear away at our well-being, our intelligence, and in some cases, our lives, but should instead use it to empower, to spread awareness, and to educate ourselves and others, in our lives and around the world.

Why?

Because it's the feminist thing to do.

PART FIVE

GLOBAL MISOGYNY:

THE COLD, HARD FACTS

What exactly *is* happening to the women of our world? Statistics are thrown around, and news stories crop up every once in a while, but the way our media works, the reality of global misogyny isn't exactly front-page, daily news. And for some reason, most grade schools' curriculums consider the centuries-old battles between white guys far more important than the atrocities being committed against women as we speak.

So I'm going to try to make up for those gaps. I'm going to try to give you an essential guide to what really is happening to women around the world—and why feminists care.

The stark truth is that *millions* of women are suffering from oppression, violence, and/or abuse every single day of their lives.

According to a United Nations study done in 2006, at least one in every three women worldwide (that's about one billion women) have been beaten, coerced into sex, or otherwise abused in their lifetimes.[1] Research also shows that women make up 70 percent of the world's 1.3 billion poor and own only 1 percent of all land in developing countries. (This phenomenon has been dubbed the "feminization of poverty.") Beyond the horrific implications of such dire poverty, the same research shows that there is a correlation between poverty and domestic violence: The poorer the nation, the more women are victimized by domestic violence.[2] And these are just a couple examples of the way women are treated due to inequality.

This shit is *real*. It's so real. It's happening right now, as you read these words. It took a lot for me to really, truly, deeply realize that—to fully wrap my mind around the fact that there are women out there who are mutilated, murdered, *buried alive*—all essentially because they're female.

It's amazing to me that this can happen. That women are abused and brutally harmed in a variety of ways in every country in this world. That people can still deny that it's happening, or can simply put it on the backburner in terms of their priorities. It's amazing to me that the people who want to help them—feminists and humanitarians—are belittled and told that their work is useless and not needed, told that everybody is already equal. But that too is reality.

Another unfortunate truth is that this section could be virtually endless. It deserves its own book, and in fact, there already are many great books on global misogyny. But I'm going to focus on four very pressing and very serious issues that women and girls across the globe are facing today: sex trafficking, female feticide and infanticide, female genital mutilation, and honor crimes.

I've said it before, and I'll say it again: This is just a *small sample* of the gross smorgasbord of atrocities that are committed against women daily. But I think it's enough to provide a window into what's happening.

SEX TRAFFICKING

What do you picture when you read these words: "one of the most profitable enterprises in the world"?

Industry, progress, innovation? Towering high-rises all over the world's capitals, all bearing the same logo? An unbelievably wealthy CEO sitting back and enjoying fine wine on his private jet? The thousands and thousands and thousands of employees who work for him (yes, him)?

Let me correct you. Imagine instead a girl, eleven years old—maybe even younger—who is scared, alone, beaten, and abused. Imagine a young woman being persuaded by a seemingly trustworthy man that he has work for her—a cleaning job, a restaurant job—that will help her feed her starving family. Now imagine that young woman being kidnapped. Imagine her being shipped to a foreign country where she knows neither the language nor another living soul. Imagine her beaten into submission, and then forced to sell her body, all proceeds of which go to her kidnappers.

This is what sex trafficking looks like, and it's one of the most profitable commercial enterprises in the world. It is the largest subset of human trafficking, which has an estimated worldwide value of more than US$32 billion and which is the second-largest source of revenue for organized crime in the entire world.[3] Between 600,000 and 800,000 people are trafficked across international borders every year.[4] About 70 percent of them are trafficked for prostitution or other forms of sexual exploitation.[5]

If this is news to you, you're probably burning with questions right now. Which is something I can understand, because I was in the exact same position not so long ago. Now, I'm not an expert, but I'll try to give you some basic answers.

So how does this work? How, in this day and age, can people actually enslave others?

The truth is, almost every country in the world is involved in human trafficking.

Countries can either be a "source" (where people are kidnapped) or a "destination" (where they are exploited for profit via brothels, strip clubs, escort services, or, in the nonsexual cases, slave labor).

Source countries tend to be economically and politically unstable, because such environments breed "push factors"—that is, reasons why people there want to leave, to escape their existing circumstances. Push factors include poverty, a lack of a sustainable income, political instability, and social oppression. There are also "pull factors"—reasons why people can be enticed to leave for a destination country, such as the perception that life will be better, or they can easily earn money to send home to their families. Traffickers exploit these pull factors by designing ads targeted at women and offering work in destination countries. Women take these positions hoping for a new start in a place they see as a practically utopian alternative to their current lives. They don't find out the truth—that they were trafficked—until they arrive. And this is all assuming that the woman is trafficked (semi)voluntarily. Many boyfriends, husbands, and families sell their significant others and daughters into human slavery against their will, seeing the immediate payment as worth the emotional loss.

Destination countries, such as the United States, are usually developed countries that to some extent tolerate the presence of sex industries. While such industries and practices may be illegal in destination countries, little is done to truly put a stop to the institutions, which ultimately allows them to flourish.[6] In 2005, the U.S. State Department's Office to Monitor and Combat Trafficking in Persons estimated that between 14,500 and 17,500 people are trafficked into the United States every year.[7]

But why don't they escape? There must be some way for these women to find a way out, right?

Unfortunately, pimps have found more ways to imprison their human commodities than just chaining them down. Debt bondage is a popular method of imprisonment. People who have been trafficked are told that they owe their pimps money for food and board. Conveniently for the pimps, the amount owed is *always* more than the money earned by each woman—no matter how much is earned—so they are constantly in debt, and thus, stuck. Pimps also threaten to reveal their prostitutes' illegal immigration status, which would crush their dreams of starting a new life, not to mention the frightening legal consequences. Some pimps choose to force their prostitutes to consume drugs and alcohol, so that once the women are addicted, they find it impossible to leave the person who has become their source. Of course, psychological and physical abuse is still liberally employed. Pimps dehumanize their prostitutes—verbally, physically, sexually, and emotionally—to the point where they value themselves so little that they have absolutely no confidence to attempt to escape.

Leaders of developed countries must be against this. Why aren't they doing anything about it? Why aren't they stopping it?
Essentially, sex trafficking is incredibly complex. It is caused by a huge web of interconnecting and interdependent factors. To stop sex trafficking, we'd have to unravel this web. Such an effort would require a massive amount of resources and attention from governmental officials from across the world. It would have to be a priority across the board in the context of global politics.

Let's just say it's not.

Source countries and destination countries would have to work together for the greater good of millions of women and, in many cases, would have to put aside longstanding conflicts and rifts.

Let's just say that doing so is also not a priority for today's governments.

It's also undeniable that if this web should be broken (god willing), we'd also have to create a huge support system for the people who were once entangled. You can't completely destroy an individual's environment—no matter how degrading and dangerous that environment may have been—and then set her free without support structures in place. To do so would be horribly detrimental.

Here's an example. Imagine a woman from Thailand is trafficked to the United States when she is fourteen years old. Imagine that for years, her pimps physically and verbally abuse her, that she's repeatedly raped on the job and is forced to become addicted to heroin to ensure she'll never leave. Then imagine that somehow, she's miraculously freed. Now what? She has no money and no skills. She's uneducated. She's addicted to heroin. She barely speaks English. And on top of everything, she's still probably suffering from the impact of years of abuse. So she's free. But what does that even mean?

See what I mean? It's complicated shit.

But there must be something constructive we can do about this. There must be some kind of step we can take toward creating a solution, right?

Well, I think one such step is including more women in politics—not just in our country, but in the world. I'm not talking about politicians like "don't retreat, reload" Palin or "not all cultures are equal" Bachmann. I'm talking about female politicians who are passionate about women's issues and want them on the agenda.

Because getting more women into politics isn't just about patting ourselves on the back. It's not about being able to say, "Look at the progress we've made! Look how equal our society is!" No, getting more women (and again, by "women," I mean "women who actively support women's issues and promote agendas that benefit women") into politics is essential for making strides toward greater solutions.

Of course, we shouldn't discount male politicians who do understand this dire situation and who want to fight on behalf of these women. They are incredibly important too. But getting more women into politics means having political representatives who can more directly relate to the plights of women across the world and who can therefore better represent them.

Yes: I think that having more female politicians is potentially the difference between life and death for women across the world.

However, for a more immediate way to get involved, a great place to start is learning more about organizations that currently work to fight human trafficking—like the Not For Sale Campaign (see Resources).

FEMALE FETICIDE AND INFANTICIDE

When we speak about Southeast Asia and China, it's usually to note the economic progress and continued growth in the regions. Their financial prowess has the West shaking in its boots. And they're outperforming us in other ways too: In 2010, Chinese students scored higher on an international standardized test than U.S. students by a wide margin.[8]

Behind this progress, however, lies a dark secret: At this very moment, thousands of women from China and Southeast Asia are killing their baby girls, or already have. What's worse: The practice is not only normalized, but also largely accepted as inevitable.

Female feticide is the act of purposefully aborting a female fetus because it is not male. Female infanticide is the murder of a female infant under twelve months due to sexist beliefs. In India, commonly practiced methods for killing female infants include strangulation; starvation; feeding them dry, unhulled rice that punctures their windpipes; forcing them to swallow poisonous powdered fertilizer; and smothering them with a wet towel.[9] The origin of the revolting practice of female infanticide dates back at least to the early nineteenth century, but probably goes back even farther. In 1834, it was recorded that the entire city of Bombay had a mere 603 girls, and in some Indian villages, no girls were found at all.[10] Today more than 50 million girls are missing in India due to female feticide and infanticide.[11] What's worse, this number is going up, from 25 million missing in 1990 and 35 million in 2001.[12]

In addition to the horrific act itself, female infanticide and feticide is creating increasingly skewed ratios of men to women.

In South Korea, 30,000 female fetuses (about 1 in 12) are aborted each year, despite the fact that abortion and disclosing the sex of a fetus are both illegal. This results in a sex ratio of 116 boys born for every 100 girls—one of the highest ratios of any country in the world.[13]

According to a 2011 census done by the Indian government, the overall girl-to-boy ratio in India is 940 : 1000 (the average global ratio is 984 : 1000) and descends to as low as 818 : 1000 in Chandigarh, the capital of two northern states, Haryana and Punjab.[14] What's scarier is that this gap seems to be widening over time: The same census shows that the ratio for children under seven years of age has been sharply declining since the 1960s and is, as of 2011, at 914 : 1000.[15]

As these children grow older, more serious problems ensue. It's estimated that between 30 and 50 million Chinese men of marrying age could find themselves without a spouse in the next two decades, according to Professor Li Shuzhuo of the Institute for Population and Development studies at Xi'an Jiaotong University.[16] And according to researchers at the Chinese Academy of Social Sciences, this upsetting occurrence has prompted another equally troubling phenomenon: As a result of a lack of women, forced prostitution and human trafficking have become rampant in some parts of China.[17]

Also in China, there are multiple communities of "bachelor villages," populated with single men who are unable to find wives—women who are "missing" from their country due to practices like female feticide and infanticide.[18]

Why would people kill their own babies and fetuses just because they're female?

Female feticide and infanticide are generally, though not exclusively, practiced in rural areas, because in such areas, men are far more valued than women. Why? Because men earn money for their families, while girls inherently cause their families steep financial blows. Girls are seen more as a liability than an asset. According to a 2003 interview with, Rishi Kant—founder of the Shakti Vahini Law Network—a woman in rural India could be bought for 4,000 rupees (US$80)—less than the price a cow.[19]

Also, if an Indian family wants to uphold its name in the community, it must pay a significant sum of money (called a dowry) to the man who is going to marry their daughter. The cost of a dowry, combined with the cost of an actual wedding, which the bride's family is also responsible for funding, can easily amount to as much as one million rupees, whereas the average civil servant makes only about 100,000 rupees (US$2,000) a year. In some cases, families who fail to provide dowries for their daughters are actually murdered.[20]

But the practice of feticide and infanticide in India runs deeper than this surface misogyny of male-preference. No, to truly understand why these women kill their own daughters—and why this is not merely about men oppressing women—we need to consider the life of a woman in rural India: Poverty is crushing. Women are abused and treated like slaves or livestock. In some families, women who outlive their husbands are denied inheritance and are banished from their homes. Many of these outcast widows end up begging on the streets.[21]

When women must endure such a horrific lifestyle—and when it seems there is no hope for anything better—it's almost understandable that they often deny their own daughters life itself.

Consider the case of one such Indian woman: Lakshmi, from the state of Tamil Nadu. After giving birth to her second daughter, she refused to nurse the infant for three days, then poisoned her. Lakshmi's female neighbors helped her bury her child in a small hole near her home. When asked how she could do such a thing, Lakshmi responded, "Instead of her suffering the way I do, I thought it was better to get rid of her."[22]

But this is murder. It must be illegal. What is being done to stop this?

In the past two decades in China and India, the use of ultrasound machines to reveal a child's sex has been made illegal. In fact, in 2002, India strengthened the restrictions by including penalties such as three years in prison and a US$230 fine for the first offense, and five years in jail and US$1,160 for the second offense.[23] However, this has hardly restricted the prevalence of parents using ultrasounds to discover the sex of their fetus. Many Indian women still visit local health centers where abortions and the illegal use of ultrasound machines occur daily. In fact, there are practices that profit almost entirely from doing sex-selective abortions. According to a 2006 *Washington Post* article, some clinics at the time were offering an ultrasound-plus-abortion package, which retailed anywhere between US$80 and US$230.[24] Entrepreneurs have been known to keep ultrasound machines in their vans and visit rural communities.[25]

While government officials in India haven't necessarily ignored this practice, attempts to end it have failed. In 1992, the Indian government announced the Jayalalitha Protection Scheme for the Girl Child—the goal of which was to totally eliminate female infanticide by the year 2000 by offering monetary incentives to poor families who had one or two daughters, and no sons, as long as one parent agreed to be sterilized. In 1997, the Indian prime minister announced a similar program for the entire country. However, while noble in theory, the incentive program is not as widespread in practice as the government had hoped it would be. It also does little to address the root of the problem, which goes beyond poverty.[26]

What about a woman's right to choose? How do I rectify that with an Indian woman's choice to abort girls, horrible as it is?
I support a woman's right to choose. But I do not support aborting fetuses simply because they are female. I see how the involvement of abortion in this practice may complicate things, but I'm not opposing a woman's right to have an abortion *at all*. Rather, I am opposing the way it is being used in this instance. The bottom line is, girls are being murdered because of their gender, which is not only wrong, in and of itself, but which is also reflective of deeply misogynistic values.

FEMALE GENITAL MUTILATION

Throughout the world, young women from all kinds of cultures experience a rite of passage: a milestone, event, act, or ceremony that signifies that their childhood is ending, that they are becoming a young woman. There is not one definitive rite of passage in the Western world, but it might be, for example, starting your period. Or buying your first bra.

For girls in parts of Africa, and in some other parts of the world, the major rite of passage is a practice called female genital mutilation (FGM). And the practice is as absolutely terrifying as it sounds. The practice of FGM can be classified into three categories: clitoridectomy (the partial or total removal of the clitoris), excision (clitoridectomy plus the partial or total removal of the labia), and infibulation (narrowing or covering the vaginal opening, which involves repositioning the labia

VIOLENCE AGAINST WOMEN: FACTS AND FIGURES

One of the main things all feminists can agree on is that violence has to stop. When you really look at the statistics, it's actually insane—and really, let's just say it, primitive—how much violence there is in the world.

Maybe we can't all fly to foreign countries and attempt to help every woman in the world. In fact, maybe we shouldn't. The imperialistic implications of doing so may be problematic enough in their own right. But there's one very important way we can all work to combat these injustices, and that's raising awareness and educating ourselves.

PHYSICAL VIOLENCE[27]

- Worldwide, at least one in three women and girls is beaten or sexually abused in her lifetime.

- More than 90 million African women and girls are subjected to female circumcision or other forms of genital mutilation.

- In Zimbabwe, in the high court in Harare, domestic violence accounts for more than 60 percent of murder cases.

- Boys who witness their father's violence are ten times

and which can include a clitoridectomy).[29] The term "cutting" (and "female genital cutting," or "FGC") is often used instead of "mutilation," which can be seen as disparaging to survivors of the practice. According to a 2010 World Health Organization study, approximately 100 to 140 million girls and women currently live with the consequences of female genital mutilation, not least of which are health-related: infection, cysts, infertility, blood-borne diseases, increased risk of childbirth complications, and even death.[30]

more likely to engage in spousal abuse as adults than boys from nonviolent homes.

- Somewhere in America, a woman is battered—usually by a partner—every fifteen seconds.

SEXUAL VIOLENCE[28]

- Four million women and girls (of which about one million are children) are trafficked annually.

- In eastern and southern Africa, 17 to 22 percent of girls ages fifteen to nineteen are HIV-positive, compared to 3 to 7 percent of boys of the same age. This pattern— seen in many other regions of the world—is evidence that girls are being infected with HIV by a much older group of men.

- In the United States, 17.6 percent of women have survived a completed or attempted rape. Of these, 54 percent were seventeen years old or younger. The FBI estimates that only 37 percent of all rapes are reported to the police, while the U.S. Justice Department places the figure even lower, at 26 percent.

- Approximately one in five female high school students report being physically and/or sexually abused by someone they've dated.

Who is doing this to young women? Where is this happening?
Female genital mutilation is predominately practiced in twenty-eight African countries, although it is sometimes practiced in Asia, and cases of it have been reported in parts of Europe, Australia, Canada, and the United States (in those countries, the cases mostly involve African immigrants).[31] Most Africans who perpetuate FGM are also Muslim, though there are African Christians who do it too.[32] Though FGM is often associated with Islam, this is in fact a misconception. Neither the Koran nor the Sunnah (the two major

sources of Muslim law) dictate FGM, and most Muslim scholars agree that it is not a religious requirement.[33]

The specifics of the practice vary greatly, depending on the individual culture. For example, in Yemen, girls are typically cut within two weeks of birth, whereas in Egypt, FGM can occur in a woman's early teenage years.[34] Surprisingly enough, the actual act of cutting is usually (but not always) performed by other women. It is often a duty passed down from one generation to the next. Many cutters learn the technique from their own mothers or grandmothers. In these cases, sterile blades are not always used (and, thus, the surgery often causes infections or spreads diseases like HIV), and the practitioners are generally not trained in how to stop excessive bleeding. Traditional birth attendants do the cutting in some countries, whereas in others, a woman who belongs to the blacksmith caste will perform the procedure. Still in other countries, medical professionals will even perform FGM.[35]

Why would anyone do this to young women?

Some cultures that practice FGM claim it is beneficial for women's health and well-being. From a medical perspective, this is unequivocally false. As I mentioned earlier, female genital mutilation can result in irreversible lifelong health problems.

Other cultures perpetuate FGM simply in order to control female sexuality or, essentially, promiscuity. Such cultures have rigid beliefs about what constitutes "proper" sexual behavior (specifically, what is proper for women). They believe that by cutting a woman, they will reduce her libido, which will in turn decrease the chance she will engage in pre- or extramarital sex. Infibulation, in which the vaginal opening is covered or narrowed, serves as an indicator of virginity or faithfulness. For women who have been infibulated, intercourse would not only painfully open the wound but would also be a clear marker of "illicit" behavior—behavior that would be severely punished.[36] In these cultures, trusting women with their own, unharmed bodies—let alone allowing them to freely explore their sexuality—is not an option.

In most cultures that practice FGM, it has been done for so long that it's become a cultural staple and is accepted as a concrete part of life. In many places, it is considered fact that in order to properly raise a daughter, she must undergo cutting. For parents in these communities, to deny this rite of passage would be to fail their daughter, to fail to prepare her for adulthood, womanhood, and marriage.[37]

Is anybody doing anything to stop this?
Interestingly enough, some countries where FGM is practiced have had laws against it for decades.

In Sudan, a law was passed against infibulation in 1925, and it was extended to all female genital cutting in 1946. In the 1960s, Guinea passed a law that punishes female genital mutilation with a life sentence of hard labor, and if a woman dies within forty days of being cut, the law says that the perpetrator should be sentenced to death. But these laws have done nothing. In Sudan, more than 90 percent of girls are still cut, and despite the fact that 99 percent of Guinean women have been cut, no case against a perpetrator has ever come to trial.[38]

The Western world is not lacking in declarations against this practice either. Major humanitarian organizations, including the United Nations, have actively opposed the practice for years.[39]

We can denounce the practice, and governments can pass all the laws they want, but without educating the people of the cultures who commit these humanitarian crimes, these words will do little good. Merely telling people their cultural practice—a practice they take pride in—is "wrong" is wildly ineffective. Instead of resonating, it becomes an imposition and usually results in people from these cultures feeling attacked and defensive.

How can we teach those practicing FGM about its harmful and inhumane consequences?

This is far from being cut-and-dry. First off, it's essential to consider *who* will be doing the educating, and in what way. We in the West may have great intentions in trying to reach out to women and men and to dissuade them from engaging in the practice, but the fact is that FGM is not a part of our culture. We may be able to teach those who practice FGM about the issues, but the perspective we're trying to force on them will always be the perspective of an outsider.

Many activists now believe that the best way to end FGM is to empower the women in those cultures practicing it. Tostan (www .tostan.org) is a West African group that does just that by placing FGM in the context of community development and educating African women about it in a holistic and participatory way. Tostan's educational sessions are conducted in local languages and are instructed by trained local staff. Instead of telling the women what to do, Tostan merely presents them with as much information as they can and urges them to make the best decision for themselves.

Molly Melching, the founder of Tostan, is a firm believer in empowering African women to make their own, informed decisions about FGM, as opposed to Westerners trying to dictate their actions. "When the history of African development is written, it will be clear that a turning point involved the empowerment of women," she said. "Tostan has demonstrated that empowerment is contagious, accomplished person by person, and spreading village by village."[40]

HONOR CRIMES

I don't think our generation realizes how much we've benefited from the sexual liberation earned by second-wave feminists. Sure, there's still a lot of puritanical bullshit that we still haven't erased— for example, the virgin–whore dichotomy, the double standards around sexual promiscuity (men are "players," but women are "sluts"), and the persevering existence of abstinence-only sex education. We may have a ways to go before we're a society that no longer associates sex with shame or moral shortcoming, but at least we're not a society that kills in the name of purity.

In 2010, a sixteen-year-old Turkish girl was buried alive by her own family.[41] Why? She had male friends. Allegedly, after she was seen talking to peers of the opposite sex, her grandfather and father tied her hands together, forced her to sit in a hole they had dug, and filled the hole with soil, murdering their own daughter and granddaughter.

This is not an isolated incident. According to the website of a United Nations organization, as of 2000 there were an estimated 5,000 so-called honor killings committed every year.[42] Even that horrifying number is said to be a low estimate, as many killings are disguised as accidents or suicides. And that number doesn't include the occurrence of honor rapes or beatings.[43]

Honor crimes—which are generally murders, beatings, mutilations, or rapes—essentially occur if a woman is suspected of having lost her sexual "purity." In the cultures that practice it (virtually all are Muslim cultures, most notably in Pakistan, Turkey, Jordan, and Syria), a woman's chastity is directly related to her family's honor. If a woman has risked her chastity, then her family loses face within the community, which is unacceptable.

Most people assume that all targets of honor crimes are women who—out of either love or lust—make the personal decision to have forbidden sex in a repressive culture. And that alone is enough to horrify. But often, women are the targets of honor crimes because of *other* crimes that were committed *against* them. What most people don't realize is that rape survivors are also targeted for honor crimes, as are girls and women who have been abducted or arrested, lawfully or not.

Why aren't women in these countries speaking out against this custom? Why aren't they taking action?

Well, there's the obvious paralyzing fear that must accompany the thought of standing up to people (in many instances, your own family members) who would actually murder you just for talking to the wrong person, let alone directly rebelling against their values.

And that's just assuming that these women actually do believe that honor crimes are wrong. I don't want to speak for these women, because I have no idea what it's like to be them. But I think it makes sense that if everyone you've ever known believes that women deserve to be severely punished or killed for dishonoring their families, it's not so improbable you might agree. And even if women in these cultures do believe that honor crimes are wrong, who the *hell* is going to stand up for what's right?

Just like with sex trafficking and female feticide and infanticide, the roots of honor crimes are deeply embedded into the culture in which they occur. To end such a practice would, unfortunately, take a lot more than a strong, brave group of women standing up to it.

GETTING INVOLVED: WHERE ACTIVISM MEETS IMPERIALISM

It's natural, after learning of these realities, to want to do something. It's hard for any rational and compassionate human being to know that people are hurting, that human rights violations are occurring with frightening regularity. It's hard to know that you're going to continue on with your life while women continue to be treated this way around the world.

But it's also hard to know what exactly you *can* do. You may watch *CSI* like it's your job, but I'm guessing that it is, in fact, *not* your job, and that you can't exactly go out and initiate a crackdown.

I'm also guessing you don't have the financial means to fund a humanitarian mission to any of these countries.

And even if you could do those things, the fact is that trying to do something about these complex issues can get pretty complicated. Something that feminists struggle with a lot, in terms of trying to help their sisters around the world, is the issue of being imperialistic in our attempts to administer aid. It's all too easy to view the victims of these occurrences as people who need to be saved. It's all too easy for us to think we can swoop in, that we can put on our hats of Western superiority, load up some Uzis, and shoot shit up (the American way) until we've saved these women. We may have the best intentions in wanting to use what we see as superior resources to do good in this world.

But a lot of people argue that it really isn't our place to save anybody else, and that to do so would be verging on imperialism, no matter what our intentions.

I'm the kind of person who likes to be upfront about my short-comings, intellectual and otherwise. (No, seriously, ask me to do your laundry *without* shrinking it or turning it another color. Or give me a protractor and watch me go—or rather, watch me try to turn it into an accessory, because I have no idea what else to do with it.) And this is definitely an area where my knowledge falls short. So, to sort through this issue, I turned to an expert.

I asked Feministing blogger, brilliant author, and my personal feminist sensei Courtney Martin how young feminists should approach the conflict between wanting to put their activist spirit to work and encroaching on a weird imperialistic dynamic.

According to Sensei Courtney, it's understandable that feminists feel paralyzed by guilt at the disparity between our own relatively blessed lives with, say, a woman who is stoned to death for having an affair. But if we want to get to a place where we can figure out how to help, we need to get over this paralysis. Said Courtney,

"I think it's fine if you feel guilt—that might be an actual reaction, that might be something to process for yourself. But ultimately, that emotion is so destructive when it comes to actually collaborating and making change."

And I have to agree. The most important thing is ultimately creating a world in which we'd all want to live—that's the freakin' goal of feminism after all. We can't let our own confused emotions get in the way. But how do we stop them from doing so? Courtney had some thoughts on that too:

> The thing that I always try to think of, in a very practical way, is *Am I always starting with a question?* Whether, for example, I'm donating money to women, through Kiva[44], in another country, or [whether] I'm interacting with women in my own neighborhood, am I assuming that I know what the person wants and needs, or am I actually leading with a question? Am I leading with curiosity; am I leading with the intention of being really open and trying to understand the most skillful way to be of use to people? Because I think that that's where the biggest problems happen: when people come in with unexamined assumptions about what people need and want, rather than really starting with questions and building with grassroots leaders who are already doing the work in those neighborhoods, or countries, or wherever. I think you have to be incredibly vigilant if you do any kind of activist work that includes major power differentials. Because if you're the person who's in a privileged position, you have a huge responsibility to constantly check your assumptions and privilege.

Leading with a question is probably the most honest way that we, as Western feminists, can go about examining the ways in which we can help. There should be no shame in being confused about what we can do, but there is a problem with assuming that we know what is right, and imposing those assumptions on others.

Ultimately, it's incredibly important not to victimize the women who have experienced these abuses. We use the word "victim" a lot, but I think "survivor" is probably a better term. "Victim" implies that these women are helpless, and while they may *need help*, they are not helpless. And that is an incredibly important distinction to make. These women have voices—regardless of whether they have been given a chance to use them—and we must not forget that. They, above anyone else, know best what they want to say and what they need. We, as people who have the ability to help, need to understand and respect this.

Another important thing to do is to acknowledge what is in fact happening in our own backyards. This is something I've had to work on. In the past, when I was questioned or challenged about my feminist identity, about the movement itself, or about the need for feminism in today's modern world, it always used to be the global feminist issues that grounded me. "You don't think we need feminism anymore?" I'd say. "If we write off feminism, where does that leave the young girls in rural China who will never attend school? Where does that leave the women in the Sudan who are 'ruined' or subjected to rape as a war crime? Who will fight for them if we retire feminism? You think we don't need feminism anymore? Tell that to the women of the world."

More than anything that was happening in my own culture, the plight of women thousands of miles away seemed more serious and caused me to feel more vigilant in my own activism. I think that this might be a common response, and a logical one at that. Compared to our problems, female genital mutilation, for example, seems to demand more attention. But I think it's also important to remember who we are, where we live, and what we *can* do. And Courtney agrees with me:

> I think part of my reaction to some of these complexities [about global feminism and imperialism] was to feel so strongly that some of the international work that we do is, in part, a way to, like, look away from the poverty

and injustices happening in our own backyards. I just feel so strongly that rather than exoticizing these inter-national issues—which *are* real issues that people need to work on—I'd love to see more feminists working really hard and vigilantly in their own communities around dif-ferent race and class issues, as an example. Because I think there's something so hypocritical about being like, "Let's save the women of Africa" when there's all this shit going on in our own backyard that we're not even dealing with.

Even if you have the very best of intentions, it can be super intimi-dating to try to help people from different social backgrounds who are so close to home. First of all, it may be disturbing, in a very personal way, for you to realize that injustices are happening so close by—that other people in the same city or neighborhood are in such dire need of help. And second, dealing with those issues face-to-face, with people so close to home, opens you up to the uncomfortable possibility of confrontation in a way that assist-ing international efforts just doesn't. But addressing the everyday problems that people in your own community face might just be the most effective way to make a real difference. And isn't such a result worth a little personal discomfort?

Everybody give Sensei Courtney a big round of applause for eloquently and intelligently breaking that down for us.

To recap:

1. Don't let guilt or trepidation keep you from doing some-thing. Actually doing something is paramount to all.

2. Lead with a question: Don't assume you know what's best, or that your role is obvious.

3. Don't ignore your own backyard: Get involved in your own community, and work on the issues that actually affect the people around you.

The final thing I'll leave you with is this: Being a feminist activist is *really important*. Actually trying to do something about these issues is vital and needed.

But don't underestimate the power of acknowledging that these things are happening, and don't underestimate the power of educating other people about what's happening as well. Acknowledging that these things happen, recognizing their very existence, is just as important as taking action against them. It's a necessary first step.

We have to do this about global feminist issues, and we have to do this about issues at home too. In our own country, we tell women who claim they were raped that they're liars, that they are to blame because they wore a short skirt, or that they should have stopped their rapists. We tell girls that they have to emulate an unattainable standard of beauty, then tell them that they're lazy and worthless if they fail to live up to these standards. We are hurt by all this, and yet we try to hide that we're hurting—which in turn leaves us to doubt ourselves, blame ourselves, and altogether feel complicit in what's happening to us.

In another country, it may be obvious who is to blame for selling a woman into slavery. We may not understand why other cultures turn a blind eye to their own misogynistic practices, or why they may even encourage them. But why is it so impossible for our culture to acknowledge our own misogynistic practices? We need to recognize that there are more parallels between our culture and their cultures. Oppression and violence against women isn't a problem constrained only to developing countries. It happens here, in our own backyard.

But whether the abuses are happening here or thousands of miles away, living in denial, and blaming girls and women for the things we inflict upon them, isn't helping anybody. It's time to be brave. It's time to be honest. It's time for recognition, awareness, and education.

But how does that translate into action you can take? Well, if you've been moved by what you've learned in this section, take this knowledge and pass it on: Tell your friends, your family, or anybody else you know who isn't aware about these atrocities. Donate your Facebook or Twitter status to describing (and linking to) an organization that works to end one of these plights, or any other social-justice cause you think is worthy. Better yet, start your own effort to fight injustice—seriously, never underestimate the power of a bake sale or a walkathon. Check out this book's Resources section, where you'll find more reading and information about organizations you can join or help.

Every person who refuses to be complacent in the face of these problems—and who does what she can to fight them—counts. So if you agree that it's time to end this shit once and for all, then take a step: Get involved and spread awareness.

PART SIX

FEMINISM:

YOUR SECRET WEAPON FOR GROWING UP

I have a deep, dark secret.

No, it's not the burning torch of fiery love I've been carrying for Michael Cera since his *Arrested Development* days. I'm very open about the fact that I believe we're soulmates, and I feel no shame in committing it to print.

It's also not my pathological fear of Furbies, nor my theory that they were dropped to Earth by an alien militia to terrorize humankind and break our spirits so that we'd be easier to colonize. I'm actually proud of that theory and am just *waiting* for the day when we're all chained together and forced to destroy our own civilization in order to make room for our new alien overlords (who, INTERESTINGLY ENOUGH, will look *exactly like furbies*). And I make no promises to refrain from performing my "Told You So" song-and-dance routine.

No, my deep, dark secret has to do with my feminist identity—specifically, that a big part of why I'm a feminist is due to pure selfishness. Yes, feminism is a movement that seeks to unite women from all planes of life, to make all of our lives better. It's fundamentally about selflessness, about doing what's right for the majority, and about helping others.

But the truth is, feminism helped *me* on a personal level—it made *my* life better. And I think it could make all of our lives better on deeply personal, individual levels. And that's probably the biggest reason why I advocate for it.

The truth is, feminism really does make you feel warm and fuzzy. I know that many people picture feminists carrying chainsaws and running around the streets seeking to destroy everything happy and good (or whatever it is people think evil feminists do), but that's just not accurate. And I know this from personal experience. Honestly, feminism helped (actually, it's still helping) me survive my teen years on almost every level.

It can be in the little things. Like in my freshman year, when I realized that I almost never raised my hand in class because I was afraid boys wouldn't think my intelligent thoughts were cute. I mean, you can only wear so much Abercrombie & Fitch to make up for being able to calculate the area of a triangle. No matter how tight your clothes, if you let it slip that you do, in fact, think from time to time, guys *will* start to realize that there's a brain floating somewhere above that midriff. The horror.

After finding feminism, though, I realized how stupid it was that I was trying to look as cute as possible for guys. I mean, these were the kind of guys who, when asked to identify what was in fact the Nile River on a map, would say, "Well, that's Scotland, and I think that water is probably the moat of an ancient castle. If you squint, you can even see the Loch Ness Monster!"

So I started raising my hand—which, though it definitely benefited me a lot, was really even more beneficial for my ridiculously frustrated teachers, who were probably starting to lose faith in humanity completely.

But the benefits of feminism didn't just make an appearance in my life in the form of an improved classroom experience. I think there are three main ways—or, more specifically, three main relationships—by which teen girls and young women define themselves: Our relationships with our female peers, our relationships with our bodies, and our romantic relationships. These three relationships help us to know who we are, how we fit into the greater context of our communities, and how we feel about ourselves. They are what truly define us.

So it's pretty problematic that my generation has a kind of messed up way of handling all three. Luckily for me, (and possibly for you!) feminism helped me navigate all three of them.

TEENAGE PROBLEM #1: GIRLS WITH FANGS

Before I even started high school, I was well warned about "how teen girls can be." But I mean, please, I had seen *Mean Girls* in middle school. It's what both initiated my adoration of Tina Fey and taught me that high school would not be sunshine and rainbows 24/7.

And as it turned out, the warnings and the movie rung true: Though middle school had its fair share of catty minibitches, their Limited Too–clad bodies really couldn't hold a torch to the girls who ran high school.

I'll be clear: There definitely wasn't a Regina George replica at my school. But there were certainly girls who made it their business to put every other girl in her place—specifically, upperclassmen who felt threatened by the incoming freshmen. I watched as freshmen girls who dared to socialize with upperclassmen boys, who walked with self-confidence, and who dared to put themselves out there were mercilessly targeted by those senior girls. A friend of mine from middle school used to walk outside to get to one of her classes every single day—in Northeastern Ohio winters, no less—because if she had walked inside, she would've passed the area where those upperclassmen girls congregated, and she was scared of what they would say and do to her.

While I largely remained untargeted by "mean girls" for most of high school, it was only because I tried to make myself invisible. Rather than being outgoing or being myself or trying to make new friends, I pulled myself in completely and stuck with people I knew wouldn't hurt me. Near the end of high school, I finally started to come out of my shell a little bit, and was promptly body-slammed by Murphy's Law when I started hanging out with a new girl who was both backstabbing and completely out for herself and what she wanted, at any cost.

We've all heard it before. Teenage girls are vicious creatures, looking only to destroy others of their own kind in order to obtain the ultimate symbol of success: the shiny, pretty teenage boy. Our wars consist of many battles that can last entire high school careers. Even in situations where peace is made, it doesn't take much for fighting to resume.

Girl-on-girl crime consists of girls tormenting other girls, not necessarily physically (although that happens too). More often than not, the torment is verbal and emotional—and relentless, lasting until the tormentor has made the victim feel practically dehumanized. It can be just the slightest comment of, "Oh wow, purple really isn't your color, huh?" to the explicit, "You're a cankerous whore who needs to back the !@#$ off." And it can go on for years. But actually, it's really hard to typify the kind of abuse that teenage girls dish out and suffer from in high school, because girl-on-girl crime is just as complex as teen girls themselves.

That's not the case for guys. If a guy punches another guy in the face and they start wrestling in a Spartan-homoerotic manner, then you know that they're expressing their heterosexual anger (ironic, huh?). But once the fight is over, it's over. If the guys were

ERIS AND THE APPLE OF DISCORD

One of the most famous girl fights of all time is part of a Greek myth (the Greeks supplied us with everything, it seems).

The story goes like this. Zeus was planning a wedding and invited everybody except the goddess Eris, who after all, was the goddess of strife, and probably would've just been a total mood-killer. Needless to say, Eris was pissed off she wasn't invited to the biggest party Olympus had ever seen. As payback, Eris created a golden apple, upon which she wrote "To the prettiest one," and placed it on the table of the wedding banquet.

At the party, the goddesses Athena, Hera, and Aphrodite—in moves of unparalleled vanity—each claimed that the apple was for her, because she was, of course, the prettiest. (Sadly enough, I totally know girls who would do this. And so do you.) They started bitching each other out ("GIRL FIGHT!"), and finally, Zeus was like, "Just shut up already, you're killing the mood," and sent them to his mortal buddy Paris to settle the matter.

Each goddess tried to bribe Paris for the title of the prettiest: Athena offered him heroic victories (as she was the badass goddess of warfare), and Hera offered wealth. But Aphrodite offered him marriage to the most beautiful woman in the world. Paris, typical guy, was like "SCORE!" and ended up marrying Helen. (Yeah, *that* Helen. The face that launched a thousand ships. This argument about "who's prettiest" led to the frickin' Trojan War.)

The moral of the story: Since practically the beginning of time, girls have been trying to tear each other down in order to be considered the prettiest, and guys have been mere tools in this battle. And also: If you're not careful, your bitchiness could cause the Trojan War. So unless you want to damn future students with the task of reading a sequel to the *Iliad,* cut it out.

friends before, they almost always go back to being friends afterward. If they weren't friends before, they move on.

Of course, that's variable, because believe it or not, guys do have feelings and are all different from each other. Some are capable of holding grudges and ending their friendships. But even if they are, it's still true that with guys, it's clear-cut. With girls, the tension is always below the surface, but with guys, it's almost always out in the open. The heartwarming story of Finneus and Bartleby (see boxed text "How Boys Handle Conflict") would be a rare occurrence between teenage girls. Conflict between two girls at war hardly ever follows a pattern that would allow there to be a neat, tidy ending in sight. Maybe it's because our problems run deeper, and have more to do with ourselves than with the person we hate. Because when it boils down to it, what we're fighting for is validation.

Take, for example, our conflicts over guys. What we're really fighting for, what we really want, is for the world to see: *Hey, somebody acknowledges that I am worth being around; that I am worth sharing a label of "in a relationship" with.* And as for the end prize—the boy we exert so much effort on winning, stomping over other girls to do so? Ultimately, that final result (the perfect boyfriend) is completely deluded and devalued—nothing more than a trophy and a symbol. We need to have a boyfriend just to know that somebody out there, in this internally pressured world we live in, is publicly acknowledging how great we are. We focus more on getting the guy than the actual relationship—so much so that the guys seem completely removed from the situation.

But that's not to excuse the guys from this vicious cycle. It's easy to believe that these boys are just standing innocently on the sidelines as girls rip each other's hair out, either totally oblivious or quite pleased. ("Oh, dude, that's hot.") But they know what's up. While they may not analyze our conflicts, or even know anything specific about them, they know that they themselves are the final prize.

Many guys are pleasantly amused by this. Who wouldn't be pleased that somebody was going to extremes to win his affection and attention? But what they probably don't realize is that they are hurt by this system too. In this system, boyfriends are prizes, sources of affirmation, and proof of status, but they are very rarely people. We completely objectify them and don't see them as what they should and really can be: a source of support, love, and friendship.

We can't expect much from romantic relationships with guys—or really even expect those relationships to be healthy—if boyfriends are merely trophies. We complain about these unhealthy relationships: "My boyfriend isn't supportive." "My boyfriend doesn't pay enough attention to me." But how can we expect them to provide us with these things when they were never really what we were going after?

And yet despite the fact that all we can hope for is an empty victory, we create intricate webs of lies, deceit, and sabotage to obtain boys. Our parents watch on, aghast, pained by the mental image of their daughter lunging at another girl for flirting with a boy she has claimed. *How did we create such a monster?* they wonder. *Is this our fault?* But even if mom and dad are fighting at home, I don't think the Art of War tactics teenage girls use on each other come from any domestic influences. Everybody always points to the media when something goes wrong with teens, and they're at least partially right when it comes to this matter.

I remember hearing, during my very formative years, about how Aaron Carter (younger brother of '90s boyband NSYNC hottie Nick Carter, and a bubblegum-pop singer himself) dated Lindsay Lohan (pre-mess) and Hilary Duff (mid-Disney, early *Lizzie McGuire*) at the same time.

The result? Lindsay began badmouthing Hilary in the press, who in turn played the victim, portraying Lindsay as an evil and possessive bitch.

Did we hear one peep about Aaron? Did anybody think to raise the point that this teen star, with his squeaky-clean image, turned out to be an asshole with polygamous tendencies? No. We were too busy buying into the idea of Lindsay drawing blood from Hilary.

That being said, the media is not the sole reason for this competitive and destructive behavior between girls. The pressure is more pervasive than that. It's pounded into our heads by our *entire society*.

The loudest message we're getting is "It's a dog-eat-dog world." And it's encouraged, and it's all around us: in politics, on Wall Street, on TV, in the movies. This "mean girl" culture we live in is just a byproduct of that message. We act out against each other because we're pitted against each other in so many different ways, and because we've been devalued—and have devalued ourselves— far too much to ever feel confirmation from within.

And it's not just boys we use to validate our worthiness. We use scholastic merit too. If we can get the best grades, that's a mark—on paper!—that will calm the swarm of doubts buzzing through our minds. If we can get that class ranking, that GPA, that acceptance letter—well, then we don't have to worry so much anymore about the world's perception of us. Somebody else, somebody we can *believe,* has documented it. (God knows, we can't actually believe it ourselves.)

This internal need to self-validate, when coupled with all of the external pressures to "be the best," leads to a dysfunctional result: Girls obsess about being "good enough" on a freakishly regular basis. We are all too aware that no matter how hard we try, we are not pretty enough or smart enough or [literally anything] enough—and that somebody else will always be "better."

Not surprisingly, the results of this obsession aren't pretty. If we know we can't be the *very best,* then all we can do is try—with everything we've got—to narrow the gap between ourselves and the "best." And sometimes that means playing dirty. *That girl has better grades than me? I have to bring her down—because I know that I couldn't possibly rise above her, or even to her level.*

How can we act like this without even considering the morality of the situation? Well, this is no longer a puritan society. Morals are a little looser nowadays. We lie on our college applications. ("I organized a fundraiser for the World Wildlife Fund" = I bought a WWF T-shirt.) We cheat on papers ('sup, Sparknotes?).

But that doesn't mean we're all bad people. We were just raised in an environment that combines relatively lenient morals with unrelenting ambition. In our short lives, we've seen hundreds of scandals played out on TV. Whether it's a politician and his favorite "escort" or bankers rewarding themselves with bonuses while we go without, we've been watching people with power do crappy things practically since birth.

Not that this complete lack of ethics is what we're *striving* for. It's just that the bar has been lowered. We've seen that people in power don't exactly get there by living the golden rule. So if we too want power, what's pushing some other girl down compared to embezzling millions of dollars?

Don't get me wrong though. My whole generation of girls isn't a completely corrupt band of bloodthirsty powermongers. There are a lot of us, probably most of us, who realize how wrong this stuff is, and how we are capable of getting ahead without tearing other people down. That's why we're not all participating in or perpetuating girl-on-girl crime. But I guarantee you that any given teenage girl in any high school in America would say they know of a girl who didn't get the moral memo—and that's a problem.

It's easy to think teen girls could and should just ignore such behavior and stay away from such girls. But it's not that simple. Ultimately, our female peers matter. It matters how we interact with them, and it matters how we feel about them. On a deep, intrinsic level, we define ourselves by the way our peers act. While

HOW BOYS HANDLE CONFLICT

There are variations, but for the most part, guys' conflicts can be boiled down to a storyline that has been in existence since those Greek guys thought to themselves *Hey, I think I'll write a play. How should I go about that?* and then created the dramatic structure.

How Boys Handle Conflict: A Dramatic Structure

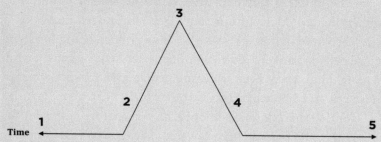

1. **Exposition: Something happens that pisses one or both guys off.**

2. **Rising Action: The guys stop talking, OR they give each other dirty looks, OR they threaten each other.**

3. **Climax: There's a fight.**

4. **Falling Action: One tells the other to stop it, and he does, OR they avoid/mutually hate each other, OR they become or are back to being friends.**

5. **Denouement: The conflict ENDS.**

Let's watch it play out between our imaginary guy friends, Finneus and Bartleby, who are on the lacrosse team and are best buds in the entire world. One could even say that they are in a bromance: They do homework together; they watch Judd Apatow movies on weekends together; they formed a "band" consisting of Bartleby on the electric xylophone and Finneus on lead vocals (recorded through a synthesizer, of course—they categorize themselves as happy/hard core/emo/electro/dance . . . with a latin flavor).

On the night before The Big Game they decide to go to their friend Ted's Super Awesome Party together. To pick up some chicas, of course.

1. Exposition (or Finneus and Bartleby Go to Ted's Super Awesome Party!)

Scene: Ted's living room. Finneus decides to go say hi to Ted while Bartleby heads into the emerging mosh pit.

Finneus: Ted, what a super awesome party!

Ted: Thanks. I think it might be getting out of control though. That spontaneous mosh pit over there is encroaching on my mom's collection of porcelain figurines. If one even gets a scratch, I'll be on lockdown until I'm thirty.

Finneus: That sucks. But it seems like everybody's having a really great time. Hey . . . is, uh, is Hester here by any chance?

Ted: Why? Are you into her?

Finneus: Hester? No! I mean, I sort of think the fact that she is president of the chess club and volunteers at soup kitchens every weekend is kind of sexy, but I am absolutely not into her.

Ted: Right. Well, that's probably good, since she looks pretty close to Bartleby over there.

(The sound of breaking porcelain emanates from the mosh pit just as Bartleby and Hester kiss.)

Ted and Finneus (*in the kind of synchronization that never actually happens*): NO!!!!

The next day—the day of The Big Game—Finneus refuses to talk to Bartleby. He's still pissed off. While he

→

→ *never explicitly told Bartleby about his crush on Hester, he suspects Bartleby has known ever since that time he forced Bartleby to teach him how to play chess, then suggested they do some volunteer work, maybe serve some soup.*

2. Rising Action (or The Great Bromantic Freeze-Out)
Scene: The locker room.

Bartleby: Dude, we're going to kick ass.
Finneus: Mmmm-hmm.
Bartleby: Did you see the guys on the other team? They don't stand a chance.
Finneus: Mmberrffm.
Bartleby: Finneus, what the hell? Why are you ignoring me?
Finneus: You know exactly what you did, Bartleby! I like Hester, and you knew it, and you kissed her.
Bartleby: Well I like her too. And I guess we know who she likes now.

As Finneus clenches his fists menacingly, their coach herds them onto the field.

3. The Climax (or Yeah . . . Just the Climax)
Scene: On the field, at the end of the game. The other team has won by one point. While the other team celebrates, Finneus and Bartleby's team walk sullenly off the field. Finneus catches up to Bartleby.

Finneus: We should have won that game. This is all your fault. You should have been watching that guy. What, were you looking for Hester in the crowd when he scored?
Bartleby: Shut up, Finneus.
Finneus: See, going after Hester screwed everybody over, not just me.

Bartleby: Shut. Up. Finneus.
Finneus: MAKE ME.

The two start beating the crap out of each other until their teammates pull them off each other.

4. Falling Action (or No More Trouble in Paradise)
Scene: The two are the last ones to get to the parking lot. Everybody else has left.

Bartleby: Dude. I'm sorry I went after Hester. I mean I didn't *know* you had a crush on her, but I knew.
Finneus: Eh. It's okay. I guess there are other girls out there.

The two bro-hug—being sure not to hold on for too long, as their very masculinity is at stake—and then hop into their respective cars.

5. Denouement (or Fight? What Fight?)
Scene: The guys are sitting on Bartleby's couch, playing Xbox. They've rented The Hangover *to bond over later.*

Finneus: Hey Bartleby? Have you seen Taryn lately? I heard she's not *that* into devil worship anymore.
Bartleby: You don't even have to say it, bro. You can totally borrow my "I ♥ The Prince of Darkness" T-shirt. Good luck!

THE END

some of us are more resistant to peer pressure, as humans, we're all basically wired to "follow the pack" on some level.

So it matters that girls often have hostile, competitive relationships with each other. And though it's really annoying and exhausting to feel like you're constantly battling people who could and should be supporting you, as we'll see below, it matters for reasons more important than that. It's messed up, and it has to change.

At least that's what feminists think.

The Feminist Solution to Girls with Fangs

So girl-on-girl crime is problematic for girls and young women on a personal level. Having to constantly compete with bitches gets pretty tiring. But while we girls have our own reasons for tearing each other down, and though it's not necessarily some conspiracy to keep women subordinate, it's undeniable that the patriarchy ultimately benefits from this dynamic. Being preoccupied with clawing at each other only makes it easier for guys to continue to hog all the power.

Basically, the feminist solution is this: The energy we focus on tearing each other down would be much better spent on trying to elevate each other. The best way for women to combat this problem—the best solution I can think of—is to join and grow the sisterhood, to embrace each other and learn from each other, rather than trying to destroy each other.

No, we're not all going to be best friends or sit in a friendship circle and share our feelings on a regular basis. This isn't an episode of *Barney*. No, this is the cutthroat world of high school. I would bet all the money in my bank account, plus a million dollars, that had you put Stalin or Putin in the bathroom at my high school, it would've taken them no longer than half an hour to come out with their arms raised, sobbing hysterically. There are no bunnies, puppies, or unicorns walking these halls. Being a teenage girl in today's society is like being a soldier on a battlefield. That is our shared experience. We're war buddies. We need to appreciate that, not make it harder on ourselves.

And why can't we just talk about it? Maybe we're not going to go up to the girl who has been bullying us since puberty and say, "Belinda. Let's talk about your passive–aggressive behavior, which I think stems from your burning desire to attend Yale and your insecurity resulting from your perception that you have a muffin top—and try to work it out." That shit could cause a mass-text rumor campaign starring you and your fictional crush on the incoherent eighty-year-old math teacher. But if we stop merely accepting these patterns of behavior as inevitable, if we start asking our friends why they think this occurs, and if we stop calling each other names (yeah, we all do it), we can cause a snowball effect. It just takes (relatively) few girls to get it started—to really commit to ending the trash-talk and the viciousness—and to inspire waves of other girls to do the same.

I know it's hard. I've dealt with some bitches in my day, let me tell you. I've had the experience of wanting nothing more than to start a rumor about, or to just bitch at, backstabbing girls in typical high school fashion. But I didn't. Rather than continuing the cycle, I always tried to move on. I may not be able to control how other girls act, but I have complete control over how I react. The power of that is continuously underestimated.

It also helped that in high school I had the greatest, tightest group of female friends ever. Knowing that I had people (specifically, girls) who would always have my back and who would be in my life forever was the single greatest thing to emerge from my high school experience. Having really authentic friendships with other girls always gave me this pillar of strength to lean back on when dealing with other girls and guys alike. I didn't have to rely on a boyfriend for moral support. I didn't have to obsess about whether or not he loved me enough, because I knew there were other people who did. And when other girls acted like bitches, I had real, healthy examples of what female friendships could and should look like. I chose really strong, unique, hilarious, intelligent girls to be friends with, and I constantly surrounded myself with them—and I think it made all the difference.

If each of us, on an individual basis, stopped our "mean girl" behavior, it would make a collective movement. It's so easy to rely on the excuse that "Nothing is going to change, so why bother?" If we're going to complain about these issues, we have the responsibility to actually do something about it. And yeah, sometimes when a girl accidentally trips you in the hallway, a crisply stated, "Watch where you're going, bitch," can feel practically cathartic. But in reality, statements like those are the very things that caused that girl to trip you in the first place. (Ahhh, see how that works?)

The feminist value of the sisterhood should also never be underestimated. We stress ourselves out by competing with each other, by comparing ourselves to each other, and by villainizing each other. I think you'd be hard-pressed to find a girl who actually enjoys this system, and yet we've all accepted it as inevitable. But the truth is, we all have the ability to end it. No, we don't have to be best friends with every other girl on this planet. That is ridiculous and unrealistic. But we don't have to be *enemies* with other girls either.

We need to correct our mindset—which has been warped by the media and by parental and social pressures—and learn who we are. If we can stop internally comparing ourselves to everybody else and start externally relating to each other, I guarantee there would be a wave of peace in girl world—one that Mother Teresa herself would be proud of.

TEENAGE PROBLEM #2: HATING YOUR BODY

When I started high school, I hated my body. I had never exactly been a stick, but near the end of middle school, I gained some weight. (Damn you, puberty, and your ability to turn delicious treats into sources of endless frustration! Damn you to HELL!) I found that I wasn't exactly fond of what my mom (in typical mom fashion) called my "curvier" shape. At the same time, my female peers began to talk about how much they hated their bodies too. They would make a joke about how they really didn't need that last cookie. They'd laugh, but their eyes would be dead serious, and I could practically see their minds working—counting calories, planning workout regimens.

I found myself doing the same things. I felt myself being sucked in. While I would never profess to having had an eating disorder, I engaged in behavior that was certainly disordered in the sense that it interfered with the way I lived my life and prohibited choices I otherwise would've made. Essentially, I developed routines that maintained negative views of my own body. I avoided shopping at all costs, lest I was forced to try on a size larger than I felt I should be. I wouldn't let myself get too close to anybody else, somehow convinced that the closer I got, the more magnified my flaws would seem—which would inevitably lead to rejection. I thought about the calories in every item of food I put in my mouth, then felt horrible for hours afterward. So though I never had an eating disorder according to clinical definitions, and though I never did anything to make myself lose weight, it wouldn't have taken much to get me there. And living that way was a fucking nightmare.

Our relationships with our bodies have a great power over us, and I don't think even we understand the full extent of it. We use our bodies to project an image of who we want to be into the world. And the way that people react to our bodies hugely defines how we in turn feel about ourselves. If a guy thinks we're hot, we define ourselves as "desirable to men." We learn how girls who are desirable to men behave from the media and from our peers, and then we emulate that behavior. We become that persona. And at the other end of the spectrum, girls who are told that they are undesirable learn that they are less valuable to others, and value themselves less.

Self-image has a huge sway over who we are, what we do, how we behave, and who we become. Teen girls who learn they are conventionally beautiful may find that they don't have to develop their intelligence or their sense of humor, figuring that being beautiful in this society is more than enough to get them whatever they want. They deprive themselves and others of the greater person they could've been. Teen girls who learn that they are conventionally unattractive restrict themselves and their development just as thoroughly, deducing that they have a major flaw and are thus fundamentally unworthy. They hide, because they feel that's what society asks them to do. And that's what the media does by failing to represent them.

And there's another problem with this equation: The way we feel about ourselves doesn't even necessarily have anything to do with how we actually look. I'll never forget the day I realized this. It was the middle of my freshman year, and I found myself alone in the bathroom with the most beautiful and popular girl in the senior class. Since I was a freshman—and the kind of girl who read books like the *Second Sex* for fun and who thought wearing Chapstick was equivalent to a full face of makeup—as soon as she entered the bathroom, I prepared to leave, so that Aphrodite could descend from the pantheon to envelop this senior girl in an otherworldly glow . . . or to let her do whatever it was the pretty girls did alone in bathrooms.

But before I could leave, she blurted, "Does this shirt make me look pregnant?"

The awkwardness set in immediately. As often happens to me in intensely uncomfortable situations, I found that I couldn't speak, or leave, so I did the rational thing. I stared at her (incidentally, flat) stomach. Then a realization passed between us. We realized a code had been broken. She'd made a mistake. She'd just outed herself as insecure—and to a lowly freshman, no less. She turned her back toward me. I walked back to class.

Girls are supposed to be perfect, sure. But they're supposed to be *effortlessly* perfect, to be somehow completely untroubled by attempts at perfection. And I knew that. My generation was born with that message encoded in our DNA. But somehow it still surprised me when I saw a girl who really was *so close* to being perfect (at least to the rest of us) revealing that she was insecure—in fact, so insecure that she'd been desperate enough to seek affirmation from somebody whose opinion, at least in that context, didn't really matter.

It was eye-opening to realize that no matter what we look like, no matter how popular we are, the body-image issue among teen girls is rampant. And it's ironic. Because thanks to the first and second waves of feminism, girls today arguably have more power and control over our bodies than ever before—and yet we feel as though we have none. If we're not bingeing, purging, or exercising ourselves to death (or engaging in some combination of all three), then we can instantaneously name our least favorite body part or tell you exactly which flaw haunts us and keeps us up at night.

But our problems with our bodies are harbored less in blatant self-hatred than they are in a complete state of contradiction. Young women of my generation have a world of opportunities available to us. We can enter top colleges and later become the CEO of our own startup, or a partner in a top law firm. But we're feeling the weight of pressure and competition (coming from internal sources, such as our own high standards, and external sources, such as parents) far more than we're feeling the buoyancy of choice and freedom.

This pressure to be overachievers, academically and otherwise, is coupled with the media's constant barrage of images of unattainable bodies. In fact, teens and young adults view more than 3,000 ads per day on TV, billboards, the Internet, and in magazines, and they view more than 40,000 advertisements per year on television alone—almost all of which you can bet feature women who are skinny, tall, poreless, free of body hair, etc.[1] We're told our pores are huge and we need to buy a cream to make these things (which, excuse me, happen to serve a significant biological purpose) disappear. When we're standing in front of a mirror with our friends, getting ready to go out, we hear a girl we love and trust say, "Oh my god, my hips are huge," while another one rolls her eyes and responds, "At least your boobs are big. I look like a surfboard." We're taught that we're all just a bunch of imperfect parts that have been mashed together to create something embarrassing. We dehumanize ourselves and others. At the beach, a girl walks by in a bikini and we think, "*Somebody* should've worn a one-piece."

In these circumstances, it's no wonder that finding, developing, and maintaining a healthy body image is such a continuous struggle. We're a generation that doesn't even want to be normal; we want to be perfect. So we end up trying to live the contradiction of outwardly appearing perfect while internally feeling like a ten-ton boulder is crushing us. And our bodies and body images shoulder the brunt of this burden.

But this isn't breaking news. We've gotten to a point where we recognize that girls cumulatively maintain horribly negative ideas and thoughts about our bodies. We've gotten to the point where we recognize eating disorders as "bad." But we still haven't really understood the gravity of the situation. We look at these girls—the stereotype is affluent, white girls of the Western world (although research shows that eating disorders and body-image disorders are on the rise in non-Western societies[2]). And we think, *They're doing this to themselves. They're being prissy and need to get over*

ONE POST-IT NOTE AT A TIME

Caitlin Boyle, a twenty-six-year-old resident of North Carolina, wanted to combat the pervasive messages that our bodies aren't good enough. She decided to do a personal project: leaving sweet messages on Post-It notes in public bathrooms, at work, the gym, the mall, wherever, saying things like, "You are beautiful!" or "You're perfect just the way you are!"

Soon, having realized that affirming someone's awesomeness can have a great effect, Caitlin turned her personal project into a full-blown mission. She launched a website (www.operationbeautiful.com) that posts pictures of notes people have left, so you don't need to go to a public restroom to read these reminders and get a boost. The site also has a bunch of helpful resources, like articles on eating disorders, bullying, body image, and body acceptance.

You can read more about the project in her book *Operation Beautiful: Transforming the Way You See Yourself, One Post-It Note at a Time.*

themselves. In the scheme of things, people might roll their eyes at privileged American girls dieting to death when there are women all over the world who don't have enough food. But living in the emotional, psychological, and physical hell of an eating disorder is an oppression that should not be underestimated.

Because the truth is, eating disorders and negative body image are more than just girls feeling bad about themselves. They're breeding a generation (generations, really) of girls who aren't able to achieve what they should, who aren't able to even function the way they should, because they're so preoccupied by their bodies, and who feel worthless and dehumanized. It's a problem that's debilitating nearly half the population. And a problem that debilitates half the population is a problem that's affecting everybody.

The Feminist Solution to Hating Your Body

Now I'm obviously not the first person to reach the conclusion that a positive body image is crucial to self-realization, that an unhealthy body image stems from unbearable pressures, and that disordered eating and other obsessive behaviors are means of gaining control.

In fact, the people who reached those conclusions long before I did—and who ultimately helped save *me* from venturing into disordered eating—were feminists.

By the time I read *The Beauty Myth,* by Naomi Wolf, I'd already developed body-image issues. The book helped me understand why I felt the way I did—why society encouraged me, as a woman, to hate my body. And I began to see the situation in terms bigger than my own, personal battles. I also read Courtney Martin's *Perfect Girls, Starving Daughters* and saw so much of myself in her descriptions of those "perfect girls." It scared the shit out of me, sure, but it also really made me realize that there was so much more for me out there than obsessing over something like the way I looked (read: the way other people saw me), and that I was totally wasting my time. The knowledge I gained from those two books was powerful, and without it, I'm afraid I'd be a very different person from the one I am today. Those books helped me tremendously, and I can't recommend them enough.

However, my understanding the nature of the problem didn't make the problem disappear. Even while I was reading texts that told me I was worth more than those feelings of worthlessness, and that I was playing into society's way of controlling me as a woman, I found it impossible to alter the way I viewed my body.

Because here's the thing: Even when you come to feminism's empowered conclusions about your body—and more importantly, once you feel those realizations deeply and live those ideals—the external factors are still there. The media still streams advertisements featuring unattainable beauty standards. Peers who have not yet reached the conclusions you have reached still surround you. We live in a disordered society, and a disordered body image is our norm.

In the ongoing struggle to navigate our disordered society, gaining an understanding of the beauty myth and the nature of eating disorders is an important weapon for every teen. But it's not a solution. Why? Because understanding a societal problem doesn't change society.

For the same reason, raising awareness is great and important—but not enough. Organizations like the Girl Scouts of America, the Dove Campaign for Real Beauty, and the Dove Self-Esteem Fund have commissioned studies on girls and body image, and have made information widely available to my generation through innovative advertising campaigns, viral videos, workshops, and other resources. But in the end, the understanding fostered by these efforts has only a superficial effect. It's important to know that the media is creating an impossible situation by holding us to unattainable beauty standards, with photoshopping, airbrushing, and size 0 bodies. But the thing is, we don't need the organizations to point this out. We *know* that women in magazines are photoshopped, and we *know* that those images are unrealistic.

The real issue is that we don't *care*. We put pressure on each other and on ourselves to look that way, despite this knowledge. Why? Because real or not, these are *still* the expectations upheld for us, and if we don't live up to them, some other girl will. And for that reason, even if our teachers, parents, and other concerned adults reach out to us—tell us that we're wonderful just the way we are, that we don't have to change—it's hard to take the message to heart. Especially since their sincere messages of body acceptance don't make the competition for, say, that spot at our top choice university go away. As nice as that sympathy and comfort may be, it does very little to alter the real reasons why we torture our bodies. And as long as those reasons, those standards, exist, we're going to be doing all we can to live up to them.

I know this, because I still struggle with my body image, especially if my defenses are low. If I'm stressed about school, for example, it makes it that much harder to keep negative body-image thoughts out, because I'm already letting other negative thoughts in.

By now you must be thinking, *Oh my god, get to the point. Where's the feminist solution?*

Okay. Well, as I said before, reading texts like *The Beauty Myth* and *Perfect Girls, Starving Daughters* helps. If you ask me, it's a necessary step. You have to understand the problem. But the only way to *address* the problem is to learn to love yourself, and that's not something you can get from any book, no matter how kickass it is.

And that is where the feminist movement comes in.

Feminism is a movement based on acceptance of *all*. It's about accepting people no matter what, including what they look like. But even more than accepting, it's about embracing. And here's the thing: Before we're able to accept and embrace anybody else, we need to really accept and then embrace ourselves.

When I believed in feminism enough to define myself by it and call myself a feminist, it became apparent to me that in order to embrace others fully, the way feminism demands, I would have to learn to love myself. By learning how to cut others some slack, by learning how to really, truly accept them, I learned that it's okay to cut myself some slack; that it's okay to really, truly accept myself.

And just like with girl-on-girl crime, we seriously need to start talking about this. When girls do talk about our body issues, we tend to either totally deny we have any issues with our bodies, or act like all of us experience negative feelings, and that it's a blanket, inevitable experience. It's either, "Of course I feel great about my body!" or "Of course I hate my body! Who doesn't?" Then the topic is dismissed.

We need to start being honest and really own up to our personal, individual experiences. There are few outlets to really do this, and we need to create more. But the FBomb is one place where this happens. Body image is probably the most written-about topic on the blog. And if the FBomb is any indicator (and I think it is), girls are just dying to talk about the way they feel—the way they *really* feel. Whether it's personal tales from the front lines of high school; a critique of media images; or thoughts on beauty pageants, eating disorders, or the newest "get thin quick" gimmick, the conversations are starting. And they are conversations that we desperately need to have. I truly believe the revolution needs to come from within the ranks.

Though dialogue among my generation is crucial, there is one major way in which the older generations can help alleviate this problem. Parents—especially mothers—play an integral role in shaping their daughters' body image. I can't even count how many friends of mine have grown up with mothers who are watching their own waistlines. They've grown up around dieting, compulsive exercising, and weekly weigh-ins. Even before the media or their peers could get to them, many of my friends were dragged into the world of "body projects" by their mothers—as diet partners, as support, as the replacement "body project" when their mothers' had failed.

Positive role models are essential, and I can't emphasize enough how much it matters that our mothers feel good about their own bodies. It's not enough for our moms to tell us we're beautiful inside and out: They have to believe it about themselves too.

Of course, that's much easier said than done. While sitting your mom down and actually explaining to her how her own negative body image impacts yours is important, it doesn't necessarily mean much will change. After all, as I've said, negative body image isn't exactly easy to combat.

But don't underestimate having that talk with your mom. Don't underestimate talking about it in general. Expressing the reality of my body issues was key for me, and feminism is what made that possible. Feminism allowed me to express that I was frustrated. I never *wanted* to feel bad about myself, and I recognized how problematic it was, but had no idea how to change the way I felt. While feminism didn't necessarily offer solutions (truly learning to love your body is something that can really only come from you), it offered me a community that felt the same way. It offered me support. It offered me a way to express myself and start my own journey. And I don't know where I'd be without it.

TEENAGE PROBLEM #3: THE CONFUSING WORLD OF HOOKING UP AND DATING

The artistry that is our generation's complete construction of and approach to "hooking up" is something that continues to leave our parents baffled about whether they should be concerned or supportive—a confusion that usually renders them silent and probably contributes to their deep terror of us. It's a complex thing, and it probably deserves its own chapter, maybe even its own book (actually, there are already plenty of those). We could debate its merits, its drawbacks, methods, horror stories . . . the possibilities are endless. But instead let's examine it in terms of gender (there's a twist you didn't see coming).

But first, a caveat: I am a straight girl, and that obviously shapes my perspective on hooking up and dating. There are probably parts of this argument that apply to gay teens, and there are probably parts of it that in no way apply to gay teens. The point I'm making is that I can only speak from my own experience, so here is my personal manifesto on hooking up and dating (from a straight, female perspective).

I think hooking up can definitely be looked at as an act of feminist empowerment and a sign of gender progression. Stereotypically, women are supposed to be the ones trying to trap men into relationships. We're supposed to be commitment-obsessed, wedding-starved freaks who horde back issues of *Wedding Style* magazine like some people stash candy bars, gobbling up every last morsel on impulsive binges.

But hook-up culture proves to the world that girls (especially teen girls) are just as horny as guys (especially teen guys), and that instead of all the complications and drama that go along with relationships, it sometimes just makes more sense to—um—*express* that horniness. It also shows that girls are so freakin' busy with so many other important and fulfilling things in our lives that many of us just don't have *time* for relationships—but that there's always time for fun. Finally, women are able to make it about "just sex" (or, as the term's beautiful ambiguity allows, "just whatever it is you're doing whilst hooking up").

And that could be true. That theoretically is true. In some cases it straight up *is* true. There REALLY ARE girls who are independent and want nothing to do with relationships, I *swear*.

I'd say, however, that is the exception rather than the rule.

Hooking up—despite all of its lovely implications for female empowerment—is still a largely male-controlled practice. It's a guy's game, and even when we tell ourselves that we're doing it for us, for our own reasons, and that we feel good about it, guys are still in control. They are the ones who dictate that they will not be in relationships, but that they will hook up.

But let me reiterate again: Hooking up is not an inherently bad thing. It's actually fun, and I think girls can benefit from it, and it can be reflective of an increasingly autonomous teen girl population. There *are* girls out there who really are doing it for their own reasons, independent of any cultural or peer pressure. And that's awesome for them.

However, hooking up as a practice is largely reflective of the fact that guys are still controlling us sexually. Guys are still categorizing girls and forcing us into stereotypes in order to keep us submissive. And in a lot of situations, hooking up demonstrates how guys and girls dehumanize each other. And beyond that not being "okay" or beyond that being "antifeminist," how happy is that making any of us? Beyond thinking that it's what we're supposed to do, beyond being happy with the isolated act of hooking up—not any of the emotions or aftermath that come with it—how okay with it are we *really*?

Think about this: If guys suddenly decided that they were all about monogamy and relationships, would girls be convincing them to hook up? Would we try to preserve hook-up culture if its existence were threatened? If guys suddenly looked into the eyes of girls across the country—nay, the world even—and said, "I think you are amazing and wonderful, and I would like to focus all of my romantic energy on you, including but not limited to wrapping my arms around you and gazing at the stars on warm summer nights and writing you epic poetry to be recited in a gazebo at the edge of a pond swarming with baby ducklings," would we be like "That's nice, but I'm not really interested in that," or would we leap into his arms, screaming, "Nicholas Sparks isn't a dirty liar after all!" I don't know for sure, but I strongly suspect we'd all revert back to Saturday nights filled with double dates down at the local bowling alley and dances at the sock hop.

More often than not, even if the girl is convincing herself she's having fun (and hell, she probably *is* having fun), she's also probably hoping that something will come from it. *Wouldn't it be so nice*, she thinks, *if Finneus realized that he really does care about me, and I'm not just another random girl? I mean, what other girl can actually rival him in a Pokemon Battle? Not many! We're soulmates!*

For many girls, hooking up is the means to an end. For most guys, hooking up is hooking up.

I'm sure a lot of the desire for a boyfriend has to do with peer pressure. Even when they are participating in hook-up culture, girls still brag when they "get" boyfriends (because, obviously, it's an achievement, just like they "got" a reward—language matters, people), and they still call other girls sluts for hooking up, even if they're doing the same thing. Whereas guys brag when they hook up. Hooking up is reinforced. End of story.

Guys set the rules of the game and keep score, and if girls don't want to be alone on the sidelines, if they want to be in the game at *all*, well, then they have to play. And in order to keep the girls who play submissive, guys polarize them.

In the world of teen relationships (and I use that word broadly here), girls can be "bros" or they can be "bitches" ("sluts" and "hos" are also acceptable alternatives; I just enjoy alliteration).

She usually starts as a bitch. She is a warm body to hook up with. She is a conquest. She could actually *be* a bitch in the personality sense of the word—because what does the guy care, he doesn't exactly have lengthy conversations with her, and even if he does, he's not exactly invested in them.

This is what feminists like myself call DEHUMANIZATION, and we are not fans of it. We're objectified as a sexual pursuit, which is pretty freakin' far off from the goal of equality, and any girl who convinces herself that she's otherwise in the scheme of a hook-up with no further intentions is seriously deluded. And okay, maybe in some cases, she's dehumanizing the guy right back, using him to fulfill her sexual desires the same way he is, so she thinks it's okay, it's equal. But what kind of f'd up equality is that?

BUT. But. There is an alternative. Yes, ladies, we have two *whole* identities to choose from. Aren't we just the luckiest?

You see, girls are able to overcome being "bitches." They can be "bros." This means that they are "one of the guys." (Obviously, they can't be unattractive. Girls aren't allowed to be unattractive. Ever.) If they conform to guy behavior, they are seen as "cool" in the eyes of guys, because they act like them.

Maybe they play sports and can talk sports over a heaping burrito. (Please note that a bro must eat like a guy, but she must never gain weight. Because eating a lot or until you're full is a masculine quality. Obviously.) Maybe, while hanging out with the guys, she rates girls as they walk by. And what's hotter than a girl sexually appraising another girl? NOTHING, BRO!

The only way a girl's opinion can be respected—the only way she's actually *listened* to by guys—is if she's a bro. (A "language matters" interjection here: Women can only be respected if guys pretend that their lady-friend is also a guy by identifying them with a masculine term. Women can't be respected as women.)

So what does this look like on the inside of girl world? Well, it's really fucking annoying. Girls see their bro status as a bragging right and a point of pride. They say things like, "Yeah, I just get along better with guys. Girls are *so* bitchy and uptight and judgmental and guys are just, like, so chill." Or they coyly shrug, sighing, "Guys just love hanging out with me. I'm just one of the guys!"

When girls say things like this, it requires a lot of self-constraint; deep, calming breaths; and a countdown back from ten to restrain myself from losing my shit. I really want to mirror their coy little shrug and say, "What do you want, a cookie? A trophy? I could probably arrange for a plaque to be engraved in honor of the extreme prowess you seem to think your clearly deep and meaningful friendships with guys awards you, but the shipping on that might take a while."

One day, when I'm particularly sleep deprived, I may actually say that, but I haven't yet.

And no, that's not jealousy you're detecting in my ~~passive~~ completely aggressive natural response. It's my complete inability to tolerate the nerve that some girls have to be able to say that we're past feminism, and that we're completely equal, and then act like they are special, that it's a special achievement when guys *do* treat them with some semblance of equality—and then use it to compete with and tear down other girls. They think that their status as a bro exemplifies a status of equality, when it in fact undermines it, proving how *far* we are from equality when the respect of men merits bragging and is seen as the exception to the norm.

I mean, obviously, these are generalizations. There are plenty of exceptions—plenty of really awesome teen guys out there, and plenty of guy–girl friendships that involve legitimate mutual respect and understanding. One of my own best friends is a guy, and I can confidently say we fall into the latter category. But this is generally how our generation approaches relationships and friendships, and it is generally the way both genders interact.

And beyond hook-ups, what about relationships? Because those do actually still exist—you just don't hear about them, because the media would rather report about a group of fourteen-year-olds in a Playboy-themed prostitution ring or something, rather than, "Aw, Finneus and Beatrice just celebrated their one-year anniversary!" Blame ratings and whatnot.

The truth is, teen relationships can be really awesome, positive things for girls and guys alike to engage in. A healthy relationship—one based on mutual respect and appreciation—can be a really wonderful way for teen girls to explore who they are in a variety of ways. When a girl has a partner she trusts, one who will be there for her, it allows her (and her partner) to explore and develop a healthy sexual identity. On an emotional level, it's always beneficial to have a person in your life who you know cares about you and will listen to you. Also, having a healthy romantic relationship can make girls feel more secure in general. (Though that security may be a product of an unhealthy aspect of society that dictates that girls *must* have relationships, it ultimately allows girls to feel comfortable exploring themselves and their identities in different ways, knowing they have that pillar of a "significant other" to fall back on.)

I honestly think relationships are largely really positive things for teens to engage in. They only become problematic when one or both individuals enter into them for the wrong reasons and/or (obviously) if the relationship turns violent.

I began my first real relationship for all the wrong reasons. I was sixteen and had never had a real boyfriend before. (Sixth-grade boyfriends don't count, apparently. Whatever, those hugs and that hand-holding were REAL TO ME.) I watched as friends of mine started to date "for real," and I felt left out. I wanted to have the experience of having a boyfriend, sure. But I also wanted to keep up with them. It was also very important to me for my peers to *know* I had a boyfriend. I felt like it would legitimize my entire existence in some substantial way, like "getting" a boyfriend would just make me more worthy.

My best friend set me up with a guy she worked with. He was cute and sweet, and he seemed like he was pretty into me. That was enough. We were official after a few weeks. I somehow managed to overlook incidents, like the time I told him I was "pretty cynical," and he—clearly seeped in his Catholic-school education— responded with a wink and "That's cool, I like sinners." We dated for a few months before I realized I still felt absolutely nothing for him. It ended, and predictably, we never talked again.

Relationships like my own first one are not inherently harmful. I emerged without any deep, lasting psychological damage. But I do take issue with relationships like that, because of what they represent. Generally, they're complete products of what society expects of young girls. Girls generally enter into relationships like these because they want a boyfriend, not because they want a certain guy. They haven't found an ally, a partner, a friend. Instead, they've found a stand-in, a status symbol, and a response to a culture that tells girls that nothing is worse than being alone (read: being independent), and that it's better to latch on to any random guy than to be single.

But a truly damaging type of relationship is the abusive kind. This may seem obvious; what's maybe not so obvious is that many teens actually are in abusive relationships. One in five female high school students report being physically and/or sexually abused by a dating partner.[3] While it's true that women can be the abusers in relationships, it's also true that 96 percent of reported incidents of assaults in relationships are committed by men.[4] And abuse isn't just restricted to hitting, punching, and sexual assault. Emotional abuse—which includes putting down partners, trying to control them, and trying to alienate them from others—is a very real and pervasive occurrence in teen relationships.

One reason it's so pervasive is this: It's a common misconception among girls that controlling boyfriends are "romantic." Girls reason that if their boyfriends demand they spend time with them, and *only* them, it must mean they love them, and that they're so lucky to have found somebody who cares that much about them.

In reality, it means that that person sees you as their possession—you belong to *them* and nobody else. It's not romantic, and it's a clear-cut sign that other types of abuse may follow.

Abusive relationships are wrong for really obvious reasons. You're obviously not gaining anything from an abusive relationship. In fact you're being *harmed,* and it's very clearly detrimental. But they're also wrong because of their misogynistic implications. Abusive relationships are able to continue because women continue

PURITY BALLS

If you haven't yet heard of the freaky phenomenon known as Purity Balls, prepare yourself. Here's a description of the phenomenon, extracted from *The Purity Myth*, by Jessica Valenti.

> *Fathers escort their daughters to these promlike balls, where at some point—between the dancing, food, and entertainment (largely involving little girls doing ballet around big wooden crosses)—the girls recite a pledge vowing to be chaste until marriage, and name their fathers as the "keepers" of their virginity until a husband takes their place.*[5]

Now I don't think the choice to stay a virgin until marriage is necessarily a bad idea. It's only a bad idea when you are choosing your father instead of other men (that's just straight-up creepy) and when you're implying that anything other than what you're doing is "impure."

As if that alone weren't creepy enough, check out the father's pledge:

to be seen as subordinate to men in the eyes of a far-too-large segment of the population. Women are seen as possessions rather than individual human beings.

Again, relationships can be incredibly positive things for guys and girls alike. My second high school relationship, though admittedly short, was much better than my first. I entered a relationship with Guy #2 because I genuinely liked and cared about him. I had fun with him and felt like I could talk to him about anything. It ended, but I still look back at the relationship itself as a positive experience—one that helped me grow. And isn't that what we should strive for in any experience, romantic or otherwise?

I, [daughter's name]'s father, choose before God to cover my daughter as her authority and protection in the area of purity. I will be pure in my own life as a man, husband, and father. I will be a man of integrity and accountability as I lead, guide, and pray over my daughter and as the high priest in my home. This covering will be used by God to influence generations to come.[6]

Aside from the pretty blatant heteronormativity (again, lesbians and bisexuals don't exist), if you ask me, this idea of fathers controlling their daughters' sexuality is just plain disturbing, if not borderline incestuous. In fact, part of the "purity movement" involves encouraging fathers to actually date their daughters.

Again, it's not the concept of waiting to have sex until marriage that's problematic. It's this super unhealthy concept that girls' identities are essentially pared down to what we do with our bodies. And it's also a seriously unhealthy father–daughter relationship model. I mean, ew.

Let's just file this one under: "I Can't Believe People Think This Is What Jesus Had in Mind."

The bottom line is that a great portion of a girl's identity comes from her romantic relationships (or lack thereof). And when these relationships are problematic—when they're reflective of a sexist and still-patriarchal culture—then we need to counter them with something positive. We need to analyze them through a productive lens, and I personally think the feminist lens is ideal.

The Feminist Solution:
Hooking Up and Dating, Feminist Style

So as I've admitted, I only had two relationships in high school, but I *have* done a lot of observation of a variety of other types of relationships. I mean, it was kind of hard *not* to observe. It seems in high school, you need only cast your eyes toward the nearest secluded hallway, and there you will find the newest Couple of the Week making out. (Fun fact: If you hang around long enough in the general vicinity, you may also witness their break-up!) I also helped many friends through their own relationship issues: everything from the trials of a years-long, committed relationship to a series of random hook-ups. I doubt I helped at all (since my solution to everything was, "You should probably just eat more chocolate"), but I certainly had the opportunity to observe a variety of high school relationships and relationship-like situations.

So, how does one come out on the other side of all of this unscathed? The answer—at least for me—was undoubtedly feminism.

Feminists like sex.

There, I said it.

Feminism is largely a pro-sex movement and fosters a pro-sex culture. We're in favor of people behaving sexually. We just want this to occur in an equal way that will ultimately benefit us *all* and make us *all* happier and have better experiences.

Feminism ultimately provides a language and a structure for girls to really express what they want and need from a sexual relationship—or any relationship, for that matter. Feminism allows girls to realize that they are valuable, that they have their own needs, and that they don't have to just perform for others. It seeks to totally eradicate the virgin–whore dichotomy (that is, the mentality that girls can only be "virgins" or "sluts" and should be ashamed to be either) that haunts so many of us. As for relationships, girls are taught that they must never be "lonely." We're taught that we should always be in a relationship, just for the sake of being in a relationship, so that we can be legitimized by that other person.

But the thing about being a feminist is that it really encourages you, as an individual, to get to know and love yourself. And when you do, you'll never actually be lonely. Honestly, having that foundation of really loving yourself and being okay with being independent only makes having a relationship *better*.

Let's be honest. None of us may *need* a significant other. But it's nice to have one. It's nice to be loved and to know you have someone who cares about and supports you. And it's nice to have someone to shower with love and affection. It's actually the "needing" somebody else that can make a relationship unhealthy. When you need somebody, you cling. You pin your hopes and dreams on them. You hold them to impossible standards. And who can live up to that? It's a recipe for disaster.

Being in a feminist relationship means being in a relationship with somebody you *want*—not somebody you need. And I think that's the healthiest, happiest relationship one can be in. I think that's the relationship that will not thwart your individual identity but instead allow it to grow and thrive.

And who wouldn't want that?

FEMINISM HELPED ME, AND IT CAN HELP YOU TOO

Because of my feminist identity, I was able to dive into my teen years—a time swarming with all kinds of destructive elements—and emerge with a strong sense of self intact. Feminism helped me foster really strong relationships with other girls and encouraged me to support my female sisters rather than tear them down.

It helped me learn to love my body and to escape from the destructive, distracting cycle of body hate.

It allowed me to have healthy relationships and to know what I need in a partner, which makes for better future relationships.

Feminism has made me happier, healthier, and much more confident.

But I think more than anything else, feminism asked me to really care about myself. It asked me to take a real investment in who I am. It asked me to figure out who I am as a woman, who I am as a human, and who I am in the context of every other person on this planet.

It grounded me. It asked me to want more for myself. And before feminism, it didn't occur to me that I *could* want more for myself.

Of course, my parents told me I could be anything I wanted to be when I grew up. They totally supported and encouraged me in everything I did. And on the surface, I understood that I *could* be anything I wanted to be. But I don't think I really believed that I would.

I never thought I was special. I thought that in order to be the first female president of the United States, to be an astrophysicist, to be a novelist, even just to be loved, that I had to be special. Only special people could really be those things, I figured. And I'm just Julie.

This self-defeating ideal wasn't because of my parents. They're the best parents in the world, and they love me and always did everything they could for me. And it wasn't because of my peers either. I always had great friends. I don't know for sure, but I think this self-defeating idea about myself was just a result of being a typical girl in our culture.

It was feminism that made me realize I don't have to be special to really, truly value myself. I don't have to be extraordinary to want extraordinary things for myself. It was feminism that taught me I don't have to be "chosen" to demand more from my life, to be as happy as I can possibly be—that I just have to be here. I have to be alive. That's enough.

I've seen so many girls and guys slip into a permanent state of complacency. We adhere to stereotypes because we don't think we're capable of much more. It's easy, and we don't think we're worth it to try for what's difficult. I've watched my peers just slip by, never really discovering themselves, or even really trying to.

I want teens to want more for themselves. I want teens to care more—about themselves, about their peers, about the world. Because of my feminist identity, I do want more for myself, and I do care more. Because of my feminist identity, I'm here, and I know that that alone is enough to warrant having dreams, desires, and goals.

I'm happy. I'm healthy. I'm confident. I want more for myself. Don't you?

RESOURCES

So, you may have gathered by now that this book is meant to be an introduction to feminism. You could even think of it as a mutual friend who awkwardly (but hopefully humorously and endearingly) introduced you and feminism to each other. I imagine one of you went for a handshake and the other for a hug, and you both laughed nervously, but after a little while, you realized you have a ton in common! And you both think the other is really cool! And now maybe you want to ask feminism to hang out with you, but you're not sure how.

Well this is the resources section. Or, if we're going to continue this seriously horrible metaphor (and it looks like we are), this is where I provide you with a whole lot of opportunities to hang out with feminism in the future.

Believe it or not, there is an incredibly vast number of feminist resources out there. And I wish I could list them all. I really do. In fact, I truly agonized over which resources to include here. But unfortunately, I can only share an extremely small sampling of my very favorite feminist resources. Hopefully, this will just be your launchpad into the world of feminism. I'll let you discover the rest.

BOOKS I LOVE
The Beauty Myth
Through the lenses of work, culture, religion, sex, hunger, and violence, Naomi Wolf brilliantly defines how the "beauty myth" controls women's lives and abilities. This book will totally change the way you think about beauty—for the much, much better.

Feminism: The Essential Historical Writings
In case you didn't get enough feminist history in the first section of this book, Miriam Schneir profiles the essays and speeches of the fabulous founding mothers of feminism. It should probably be required reading for American history classes across the country, but ALAS it is not.

Feminism Is for Everybody: Passionate Politics
The title really says it all. In this book, bell hooks argues that feminism is still relevant—and relevant to everybody, despite gender, race, class, etc. Anybody who is interested in exploring the idea that feminism is the intersection of these concepts (also known as "intersectionality") should definitely check this book out.

Full Frontal Feminism
FFF is an awesome read that covers the feminist viewpoint on topics like reproductive rights, pop culture, violence, education, relationships, and more. Definitely an essential read for feminist newbies. And Jessica Valenti (the author) is a total badass.

Guyland

In this book, sociologist Michael Kimmel tells you everything you ever wanted to know about guy culture and what it's like to be a young man in today's society. If you ever wondered why guys act the way they do, find this book, and prepare to be enlightened.

Half the Sky

If you want to learn more about what's happening to women around the world, this is a must-read. *New York Times* columnist Nicholas Kristof and his wife, Sheryl WuDunn, recount their experiences on the frontlines of global misogyny and share the personal stories of women who have experienced oppressive forces such as sex trafficking, maternal mortality, and lack of education. They also make a brilliant case for why the world will benefit by improving the lives of women.

Perfect Girls, Starving Daughters

In this brilliant book, Courtney Martin interweaves personal experience with in-depth research and interviews to explore why it's so common for young women to hate their bodies. No other book quite captures the scary reality of this disturbing phenomenon like this one.

The Vagina Monologues

This is kind of cheating, because it's technically a play, but no, seriously, you have to read it—or ideally, see it performed. It's basically a series of monologues about vaginas—including the experiences of sex, menstruation, rape, birth, and more. Eve Ensler (the playwright) has also spun her creative work into a really powerful antiviolence movement called V-Day (see Organizations You Should Check Out, below).

GREAT BLOGS
Autostraddle (autostraddle.com)

I think autostraddle is one of the greatest feminist resources out there that's specifically for lesbian and bisexual women and their allies. An incredibly successful labor of love, this website updates readers about current events and other interesting news items on a daily basis. And every week, it has four magazine-style features ranging from personal essays to interviews to articles about travel, music, DIY culture, or feminism at large.

The Crunk Feminist Collective (crunkfeministcollective.wordpress.com)

While it's meant for women and men of color who came of age in the hip-hop generation, I think this blog is a must-read for any feminist-minded individual. Its mission statement is "Crunk(ness) is our mode of resistance that finds its particular expression in the rhetorical, cultural, and intellectual practices of a contemporary generation."

The FBomb (thefbomb.org)

Let's not even pretend you didn't see this coming. Yes, I probably don't need to reiterate the fact that you should VISIT THE FBOMB, but I've trained myself to take any and all opportunities to promote this blog, and I'm not going to miss out on this one. The FBomb is a blog/community for teenage feminists and focuses on an array of topics, including pop culture, sex, politics, and body image. The FBomb also takes SUBMISSIONS! Yes! You can be PUBLISHED on the FBOMB! Visit the blog for more information.

Feminist.com (feminist.com)

So yeah, the title of this website alone makes it a pretty obvious choice. But honestly, it's got some amazing resources. I remember first using it as a source for statistics (which they have plenty of) to use for countering sexist assholes' arguments that we don't need feminism anymore. They also have a whole array of columns written by prominent feminist voices. ("Ask Amy" is my favorite. I adore Amy Richards.) They also have a whole section where you can find out about feminist events and turn that feminist theory into action. What could be better than that?

Feministing (feministing.com)

Aside from being the first feminist blog I ever read (which OBVIOUSLY makes it the best), Feministing is notable for being an excellent critical feminist take on current events and is widely considered one of the founding feminist blogs. It was created by Jessica Valenti in 2004, but it is currently run by Samhita Mukhopadhyay, and it boasts an impressive list of editors and contributors.

The Good Men Project (goodmenproject.com)

It's been called "what enlightened masculinity might look like in the twenty-first century," and that is really enough to make me love it forever. The Good Men Project fosters intelligent writing and discussions about masculinity, and what it means to be a man in society today.

Ms. (msmagazine.com and ms.magazine.com/blog)

You may recognize the name "Ms." as being that of a magazine rather than an online presence. And you'd be right: *Ms.* magazine was famously cofounded by feminist activist Gloria Steinem and Letty Cottin Pogrebin and is renowned for its groundbreaking feminist writing. But good news! *Ms.* now has a thriving online presence, complete with a really intelligently written blog that covers the arts, life, health, and justice, among other important feminist-oriented topics.

Jezebel (jezebel.com)

Jezebel's tagline ("Celebrity, Sex, Fashion. Without Airbrushing") basically says it all. Definitely feminist and definitely a lot of fun, Jezebel is my absolute favorite way to procrastinate. The site's manifesto (accurately) claims that Jezebel "will attempt to take all the essentially meaningless but sweet stuff directed our way and give it a little more meaning, while taking the more serious stuff and making it more fun, or more personal, or at the very least the subject of our highly sophisticated brand of sex joke."

Racialicious (racialicious.com)

Owned and edited by the amazing Latoya Peterson (see boxed text, Part Four), Racialicious is definitely worth a read. Through the relevant and relatable lenses of pop culture, current events, and celebrities, it does an excellent job of intelligently analyzing the ways in which racism is (unfortunately) still alive and well in modern-day society.

ORGANIZATIONS YOU SHOULD CHECK OUT

In addition to the awesome organizations listed below, see Part Three for information about the Man Up Campaign (page 125), Part Four for information about We Stop Hate ("The Hate Stops Here," page 153), and Part Six for information about Operation Beautiful ("One Post-It Note at a Time," page 207).

Advocates for Youth (www.advocatesforyouth.org)

This organization revolves around the revolutionary idea that teens actually are capable of taking their reproductive health into their own hands—as long as they're given a comprehensive, positive, and realistic sex education. They also have a fabulous project called Amplify Your Voice (www.amplifyyourvoice.org), which offers a peer-written blog, great resources for teen issues, and ways to become active.

The Girl Effect (www.girleffect.org)

The About section of The Girl Effect's website explains it better than I ever could: "The empowerment of girls is the key to significant social and economic change in developing countries. When a girl has the right tools in place, a chance to use her voice, and systems set up to work for her, she will transform the lives of everyone around her. Studies show that when you improve a girl's life, you improve the lives of her brothers, sisters, parents, and beyond. The Girl Effect is about encouraging people around the world to use their voices, talents, and communities to help girls help themselves—and, as a result, everybody else. It's about providing the tools and the network needed to spread the word about what girls can do."

Kiva (www.kiva.org)

Kiva is an innovative organization that uses the power of the Internet to enable people from all over the world to lend money to international microfinance institutions, which in turn distribute this money to small businesses and students in the form of microfinance loans. Anybody can log onto Kiva and lend money (as little as US$25) to a borrower of their choice (profiles of each potential borrower are posted on the website). Eventually, once that borrower has achieved success based on the power of your loan, they will pay you back, and you can repeat the process, knowing you've made a giant difference in somebody's life for (ultimately) no cost.

Not for Sale Campaign (www.notforsalecampaign.org)

The people of Not for Sale are working hard to raise awareness about the widespread phenomenon of human trafficking, and they believe that everybody has an individual skill that best equips him or her to fight modern-day slavery. Not for Sale promotes action, and specifically emphasizes the unique ability that students have to greatly contribute to this fight. They offer a specific program students can follow to start a club at their schools. To find out more about what you can do to get involved, visit the website. If you're a student, check out their specific resources for you at www.notforsalecampaign.org/action/student.

Planned Parenthood (www.plannedparenthood.org)

This is your essential organization for reproductive rights, because the people who work for Planned Parenthood believe that a woman's right to choose will enhance the quality of life and strengthen familial relationships. Yes, they deal largely with things like birth control, STDs, and women's health, but they also offer some amazing services related to body image, sexuality, and even men's sexual health. Basically, they're awesome. Check out their website or find a center near you.

Tostan (www.tostan.org)

Based in Senegal, West Africa, Tostan focuses on combating issues such as health and hygiene, child welfare, human rights, economic development, and the environment in local communities through empowerment and education. Hundreds of African staff members (along with the support of volunteers, interns, partners, and international supporters) work to provide a holistic and participatory education to those who were previously deprived an opportunity to receive a formal education. The word "tostan" itself means "breakthrough" in the language of Wolof (spoken in Senegal), and that's what Molly Melching (Tostan's founder) and the rest of Tostan hope to inspire in the people they reach: breakthroughs in their own understandings and practices, ones they can then share with the rest of their communities.

V-Day (www.vday.org)

This is the brainchild of Eve Ensler, creator of *The Vagina Monologues* (mentioned earlier, under Books I Love). The organization is dedicated to catalyzing a global movement to end violence against women and girls, including rape, battery, incest, female genital mutilation, and sex slavery. According to the organization's website, the 'V' in V-Day stands for "Victory, Valentine, and Vagina." And if you can't get behind that, then really, what can you get behind?

The White House Project (www.thewhitehouseproject.org)

Ever notice how women are seriously lacking in politics? Well, the White House Project is all about changing that. Their mission is "to advance women's leadership in all communities and sectors, up to the U.S. presidency," because when you add women, "you get a nation that responds to challenges by drawing on the strength and wisdom of all its people, women and men."

Women's Media Center (www.womensmediacenter.com)

Believe it or not, women are ridiculously underrepresented in the media. In fact, women hold less than 3 percent of decision-making "clout" positions in the media and earned only 25 percent of all new media jobs created from 1990 to 2005—despite constituting 65 percent of all undergraduate and graduate journalism and mass-communications students. Well, the Women's Media Center is out to change all that through media-advocacy campaigns—creating its own media and training women to participate directly in media.

NOTES

Introduction

1. Carla Power, "A Generation of Women Wiped Out?" *Glamour,* August 2006, www.geneticsandsociety.org/downloads/200608_glamour.pdf (accessed September 29, 2011).

Part One: The Badasses Who Came Before Us

1. Reay Tannahill, *Food in History* (New York: Three Rivers, 1989), 6–18.
2. Ibid., 19–42.
3. Ibid.
4. Ibid.
5. "The Code of Hammurabi," trans. L. W. King, The Avalon Project: Documents in Law, History and Diplomacy, Yale Law School, 2008, http://avalon.law.yale.edu/ancient/hamframe.asp (accessed September 23, 2011).
6. Ibid.
7. Ibid.
8. Nancy Tuana, *The Less Noble Sex: Scientific, Religious, and Philosophical Conceptions of Woman's Nature* (Bloomington, Indiana: Indiana University Press, 1993), 18–21.

9. Ibid., 21–22.

10. Ibid., 24

11. Geraldine Brooks, *Nine Parts of Desire: The Hidden World of Islamic Women* (New York: Anchor, 1995), 33–54.

12. *Muhammad: Legacy of a Prophet. Muhammad and Women,* PBS, 2002. Produced by Michael Schwartz, directed by Omar Al-Qattan. Transcript available at www.pbs.org/muhammad/ma_women.shtml (accessed August 9, 2011).

13. Ibid.

14. Ibid.

15. Ibid.

16. Miriam Schneir, ed., *Feminism: The Essential Historical Writings* (New York: Random House, 1972), 6. (Italics in the original.)

17. Ibid., 15.

18. Ibid., 16.

19. Ibid., 21.

20. Ibid.

21. Ibid., 94–5.

22. Caitlin McElligott, "Women's Higher Education in the United States: The 19th-Century Debate," Miami University, 2007, www.units.muohio.edu/mcguffeymuseum/student_exhibits/site/oxford college/oxford college/WomensEdu1.html (accessed September 23, 2011).

23. "Frederick Douglass," Women's Rights National Historical Park, National Park Service website, www.nps.gov/wori/historyculture/frederick-douglass.htm (accessed September 23, 2011).

24. Miriam Schneir, ed. "Married Women's Property Act, New York," in *Feminism: The Essential Historical Writings* (New York: Random House, 1972).

25. Sally J. Scholz, *Feminism: A Beginner's Guide* (Oneworld Publications, 2010), 74.

26. Gloria Steinem, "Sisterhood," *Ms.,* spring 1972 (first issue). Reprinted in *Outrageous Acts and Everyday Rebellions* (New York: Holt, Rinehart and Winston, 1983).

27. Julie Z, "Gloria Steinem: The Iconic Feminist Speaks to Our Generation," The FBomb, March 5, 2009, www.thefbomb.org/2009/03/gloria (accessed October 31, 2011).

28. "The Pill," American Experience, Public Broadcasting System website, www.pbs.org/wgbh/amex/pill/peopleevents/e_options.html (accessed September 23, 2011).

29. Nell Greenfieldboyce, "Pageant Protest Sparked Bra-Buring Myth," *Morning Edition*, NPR, September 5, 2008, www.npr.org/templates/story/story.php?storyId=94240375 (accessed August 15, 2011).

30. Michael Neill, "The Voice of Experience," *People* 45, no. 25, June 24, 1996. Available at People.com free archive search.

31. "Current State of Teen Sports Participation," TeenHelp.com, www.teenhelp.com/teen-issues/sports-participation.html (accessed August 15, 2011).

32. "Benefits: Why Sports Participation for Girls and Women: The Foundation Position," *Women's Sports Foundation*, www.eduation.com/reference/article/Ref_Benefits_Why_Sports (accessed August 15, 2011).

33. Alison Perlberg, "Shortchanged: Women and the Wealth Gap," Gender News, www.stanford.edu/group/gender/cgi-bin/wordpressblog/2011/04/short-changed-women-and-the-wealth-gap (accessed September 23, 2011).

34. "Roe v. Wade Anniversary," Planned Parenthood of Santa Barbara, Ventura & San Luis Obispo Counties, www.plannedparenthood.org/ppsbvslo/roe-v-wade-anniversary-23556.htm (accessed September 23, 2011).

35. For more on the riot grrrl movement, check out Marisa Meltzer's book *Girl Power: The Nineties Revolution in Music* and/or *Girls to the Front: The True Story of the Riot Grrrl Revolution*, by Sara Marcus.

36. "About Us" page of the Third Foundation website, www.thirdwavefoundation.org/about-us/our-strategy (accessed September 23, 2011).

37. "Every Two Minutes," RAINN, www.rainn.org/get-information/statistics/every-two-and-half-minutes (accessed September 15, 2011).

38. "Domestic Violence Facts," National Coalition Against Domestic Violence, July 2007, www.ncadv.org/files/DomesticViolenceFactSheet(National).pdf (accessed September 15, 2011).

39. Jay G. Silverman et al., "Dating Violence Against Adolescent Girls and Associated Substance Use, Unhealthy Weight Control, Sexual Risk Behavior, Pregnancy, and Suicidality," *Journal of the American Medical Association* 286, no. 5 (2001).

40. Catherine Rampell, "The Gender Pay Gap by Industry," Economix, *The New York Times*, February 17, 2011, www.economix.blogs.nytimes.com/2011/02/17/the-gender-pay-gap-by-industry (accessed September 23, 2011).

41. "Advancing Women's Leadership," The National Council for Research on Women, www.ncrw.org/taxonomy/term/113?page=6 (accessed September 23, 2011).

42. "The United States Congress Quick Facts," updated August 28, 2011,

ThisNation.com, www.thisnation.com/congress-facts.html (accessed September 23, 2011).

43. Julie Z, "An Interview with Amy Richards," The FBomb, January 1, 2010, www.thefbomb.org/2010/01/an-interview-with-amy-richards (accessed September 23, 2011).

44. Catherine Plato, "Looking Both Ways with Jennifer Baumgartner," Curve, www.curvemag.com/Curve-Magazine/Web-Articles-2008/Looking-Both-Ways-with-Jennifer-Baumgardner (accessed September 23, 2011).

Part Two: Please Stop Calling Me a Feminazi

1. "School Enrollment," U.S. Census Bureau, www.census.gov/population/www/socdemo/school/cps2004.html (accessed August 16, 2011).

2. "The 'Truth' According to Limbaugh," Media Matters for America, www.mediamatters.org/mmtv/200508160001 (accessed August 16, 2011).

3. Dictionary.com, s.v. "feminism," www.dictionary.com (accessed August 17, 2011).

4. Urban Dictionary, s.v. "feminism," no. 85, April 10, 2006, www.urbandictionary.com/define.php?term=feminism&defid=1692832, (accessed September 26, 2011). Good news: By the time this went to print, feminists had shown up in droves to bury that "definition" with a bunch of pro-feminist definitions. That's activism at work, people!

5. In Camera, interview with Lady Gaga, SHOWstudio, August 21, 2009, www.showstudio.com/project/in_camera/session/lady_gaga (accessed October 30, 2011).

6. Sally J. Scholz, Feminism: A Beginner's Guide (Oneworld Publications, 2010), 1. (Italics in the original.)

7. Excerpts from "Interview with Gloria Steinem," conducted by Marianne Schnall on April 3, 1995, Feminist.com, www.feminist.com/resources/artspeech/interviews/gloria.htm (accessed October 24, 2011).

8. Kate Nash, "Mistakes in the Background, MySpace blog, www.myspace.com/katenashmusic/blog/447340246 (accessed October 24, 2011).

9. "Women at a Glance," UN Department of Public Information, May 1997, www.un.org/ecosocdev/geninfo/women/women96.htm (accessed September 26, 2011).

10. "Student Noses Buried in Facebooks," eMarketer Digital Intelligence, February 26, 2008, www.emarketer.com/Article.aspx?R=1005972 (accessed August 16, 2011).

Part Three: Feminists without Borders

1. "Who Are the Victims?" RAINN, June 28, 2011, www.rainn.org/get-informa tion/statistics/sexual-assault-victims (accessed October 31, 2011).

2. Peta Bee, "You, Too, Can't Have a Body like This," *The Times Online,* May 11, 2010, www.women.timesonline.co.uk/tol/life_and_style/women/diet_and_ fitness/article7122173.ece (accessed September 20, 2011).

3. "About" page of the Man Up website, www.manupcampaign.org (accessed September 20, 2011).

4. "The Case for Male Feminists," posted by Eitheror, The Daily Kos, July 10, 2009, www.dailykos.com/story/2009/7/10/752148/-The-Case-for-Male-Fem inists (accessed September 20, 2011).

5. "Fast Facts about Women in Politics," WCF Foundation, www.wcffoundation .org/pages/research/women-in-politics-statistics.html (accessed October 29, 2011).

6. Zach Wahls, personal interview, December 12, 2011.

Part Four: Feminism and the Internet

1. Trisha, "Badass-Activist Friday Presents Latoya Peterson of Racialicious," Where Is Your Line?, April 29, 2011, www.whereisyourline.org/2011/04/ badass-activist-friday-presents-latoya-peterson-of-racialicious (accessed October 24, 2011).

2. For those who have not been sucked into the YouTubiverse, the It Gets Better campaign was started by Dan Savage and his partner, Terry. In response to a slew of highly publicized suicides of gay youth, the two created a series of videos (generally personal testimonies or messages of support from allies, many of them celebrities) that essentially lend their support to gay youth and urge them to be true to who they are (hayterz gonna hayte) and that assure them that (yes, you may have seen this coming) it really does get better. The It Gets Better campaign also supports LGBTQ organizations such as the Trevor Project; the Gay, Lesbian, and Straight Education Network; and the American Civil Liberties Union LGBT project.

3. NineteenPercent, "Beyonce—Run the World (LIES)," May 20, 2011, www.you tube.com/watch?v=p72UqyVPj54 (accessed September 26, 2011).

4. "Interview with Lena Chen: Freelance Writer and Author of the Blog Sex and the Ivy," The Daily Femme, January 17, 2011, www.thedailyfemme.com/ femme/2011/01/interview-with-lena-chen-freelance-writer-and-author-of- the-blog-sex-and-the-ivy (accessed October 24, 2011).

5. "Parents: Cyber Bullying Led to Teen's Suicide," ABCnews.com, *Good Morning America*, November 19, 2007, www.abcnews.go.com/GMA/story?id= 3882520&page=1 (accessed September 26, 2011).

6. Taylor Whitcomb, "LGBT Teen's Suicide Incites Demand for Bullying Law," The Minaret Online, October 5, 2011, www.theminaretonline.com/2011/10/05/ article19558 (accessed October 10, 2011).

7. Ed Pilkington, "Tyler Clementi, Student Outed As Gay on Internet, Jumps to His Death," *The Guardian* online, September 30, 2010, www.guardian.co.uk/ world/2010/sep/30/tyler-clementi-gay-student-suicide (accessed October 10, 2011).

8. "The Truth about Bullying," Oprah.com, May 6, 2009, www.oprah.com/rela tionships/School-Bullying/10 (accessed October 10, 2011).

9. "That Facebook Friend Might Be 10 Years Old, and Other Troubling News," *Consumer Reports*, June 2011, www.consumerreports.org/cro/magazine-archive/2011/june/electronics-computers/state-of-the-net/facebook-con cerns/index.htm (accessed October 24, 2011).

10. "Emily-Anne Rigal, 17, Nonprofit Founder and Director," No Country for Young (& Old) Women, June 2011, www.nocountryforyoungwomen .com/?tag=emilyannerigal (accessed October 10, 2011).

11. "Motivating Mondays: Emily-Anne Rigal of We Stop Hate," Stop Being a Loser: Advice from Your Older, Dumber Sister, July 25, 2011, www.stopbeing aloser.org/2011/07 (accessed October 10, 2011).

12. "Hollywood's Highest Paid Actresses," Forbes.com, no date, www.forbes .com/pictures/mfl45gdgh/angelina-jolie-30-million#content (accessed September 25, 2011).

13. Sally Squires, "Peer Pressure Can Carry Great Weight in Girls' Eating and Exercise Habits," *The Washington Post*, July 15, 2008, www.washingtonpost .com/wp-dyn/content/story/2008/07/14/ST2008071401608.html (accessed September 26, 2011).

14. Christopher J. Ferguson, Benjamin Winegard, and Bo M. Winegard, "Who Is the Fairest One of All? How Evolution Guides Peer and Media Influences on Female Body Dissatisfaction," *Review of General Psychology* 15, no. 1 (2011): 11–28, www.tamiu.edu/~cferguson/Who Is the Fairest.pdf (accessed September 26, 2011).

Part Five: Global Misogyny

1. "Unite to End Violence Against Women," fact sheet, February 2008, United Nations Department of Public Information, www.un.org/en/women/endvio lence/pdf/VAW.pdf (accessed October 26, 2011).

2. "Violence Against Women: Global Issues," Feminist Majority Foundation's Choices Campus Campaign, www.feministcampus.org/fmla/printable-materials/v-day05/violence_against_women_global.pdf (accessed October 29, 2011).

3. David R. Hodge, "Sexual Trafficking in the United States: A Domestic Problem with Transnational Dimensions," *Social Work* 53, no. 2 (2008): 143. A pdf is available at www.worldwideopen.org/en/resources/detail/630 (accessed October 7, 2011).

4. Ibid., 144.

5. Ibid., 143

6. Kimberly Kotrla, "Domestic Minor Sex Trafficking in the United States," *Social Work* 55, no. 2 (2010): 181–7.

7. Heather J. Clawson, Mary Layne, Kevonne Small, "Estimating Human Trafficking into the United States: Development of a Methodology," Caliber report for the U.S. Department of Justice, December 2006 (revised), page 2, www.ncjrs.gov/pdffiles1/nij/grants/215475.pdf (accessed October 26, 2011).

8. John Hechinger, "U.S. Teens Lag as China Soars on International Test," Bloomberg, December 7, 2010, www.bloomberg.com/news/2010-12-07/teens-in-u-s-rank-25th-on-math-test-trail-in-science-reading.html (accessed September 27, 2011).

9. John Thor-Dahlberg, "The Fight to Save India's Baby Girls," Column One, *Los Angeles Times*, page 1, February 22, 1994, http://articles.latimes.com/1994-02-22/news/mn-25866_1_aid-programs (accessed October 26, 2011).

10. Adam Jones, "Case Study: Female Infanticide," Gendercide Watch, www.gen dercide.org/case_infanticide.html (accessed October 26, 2011).

11. Swami Agnivesh, Rama Mani, and Angelika Köster-Lossack, "Missing: 50 Million Indian Girls," *The New York Times*, opinion page, November 25, 2005, www.nytimes.com/2005/11/24/opinion/24iht-edswami.html (accessed September 26, 2011).

12. Ibid.

13. Sheryl WuDunn, "Korean Women Still Feel Demands to Bear a Son," *The New York Times*, January 14, 1997, www.nytimes.com/1997/01/14/world/korean-women-still-feel-demands-to-bear-a-son.html?pagewanted=all&src=pm (accessed October 26, 2011).

14. "Gender Composition of the Population," Map 11, Government of India, Ministry of Home Affairs, Office of the Registrar General & Census Commissioner, www.censusindia.gov.in/2011-prov-results/data_files/india/Final PPT 2011_chapter5.pdf (accessed October 26, 2011).

15. Ibid., Figure 21.

16. Tania Branigan, "China's Village of the Bachelors," *The Guardian*, September 3, 2011, www.guardian.co.uk/world/2011/sep/02/china-village-of-bachelors (accessed October 26, 2011).

17. "China Faces Growing Gender Imbalance," BBC Mobile News, January 11, 2010, http://news.bbc.co.uk/2/hi/8451289.stm (accessed October 26, 2011).

18. See 15.

19. Poornima Joshi, "The Cloning of Kamla," OutlookIndia.com, August 11, 2003, www.outlookindia.com/printarticle.aspx?221038 (accessed October 26, 2011).

20. See 10.

21. John Ward Anderson and Molly Moore, "The Burden of Womanhood: Third World, Second Class," *The Washington Post*, April 25, 1993. Posted on the Brooklyn City University of New York website at http://acc6.its.brooklyn.cuny.edu/~phalsall/texts/chinwomn.html (accessed October 26, 2011).

22. See 9.

23. Neil Samson Katz, "Abortion in India: Selecting by Gender," *The Washington Post*, May 20, 2006, www.washingtonpost.com/wp-dyn/content/article/2006/05/19/AR2006051901219.html (accessed October 26, 2011).

24. Ibid.

25. Rita Patel, "The Practice of Sex Selective Abortion in India: May You Be the Mother of a Hundred Sons," UCIS paper, Center for Global Initiatives, University of North Carolina, page 5. A pdf is available by searching at www.unc.edu/search/index.htm (accessed October 26, 2011).

26. Sabu M. George, "Female Infanticide in Tamil Nadu, India: From Recognition Back to Denial?" 2006. A pdf is available at www.womenstudies.in/elib/sex_selection/ss_female_infanticide_in_tamil.pdf (accessed October 26, 2011).

27. "Facts about Violence," Feminist.com, www.feminist.com/antiviolence/facts.html (accessed October 26, 2011).

28. Ibid., except for the last statistic ("Approximately one in five high school students . . ."): Jay G. Silverman, Anita Raj, Lorelei A. Mucci, and Jeanne E. Hathaway, "Dating Violence Against Adolescent Girls and Associated

Substance Use, Unhealthy Weight Control, Sexual Risk Behavior, Pregnancy, and Suicidality," *Journal of the American Medical Association* 286, no. 5 (2001). Abstract available at www.jama.ama-assn.org/content/286/5/572 .abstract (accessed October 26, 2011).

29. "Female Genital Mutilation," fact sheet no. 241, February 2010, World Health Organization, www.who.int/mediacentre/factsheets/fs241/en (accessed October 26, 2011).

30. Ibid.

31. "Facts," World Population Foundation, www.wpf.org/reproductive_rights_ article/facts#fgm (accessed October 29, 2011).

32. Nicholas D. Kristof and Sheryl WuDunn, *Half the Sky: Turning Oppression into Opportunity for Women Worldwide* (New York: Knopf, 2009), 222.

33. Jacqueline Castledine, "Female Genital Mutilation: An Issue of Cultural Relativism or Human Rights?" www.mtholyoke.edu/acad/intrel/jc.htm (accessed October 29, 2011).

34. Nicholas D. Kristof and Sheryl WuDunn, *Half the Sky: Turning Oppression into Opportunity for Women Worldwide* (New York: Knopf, 2009), 222.

35. Ibid., 223.

36. See 29.

37. See 29.

38. Nicholas D. Kristof and Sheryl WuDunn, *Half the Sky: Turning Oppression into Opportunity for Women Worldwide* (New York: Knopf, 2009), 223.

39. "UN Agencies United Against Female Genital Mutilation," United Nations Development Programme, Newsroom, February 27, 2008, http://content .undp.org/go/newsroom/2008/february/un-genital-mutilation-20080227.en (accessed October 29, 2011).

40. Nicholas D. Kristof and Sheryl WuDunn, *Half the Sky: Turning Oppression into Opportunity for Women Worldwide* (New York: Knopf, 2009), 228.

41. Robert Tait, "Turkish Girl, 16, Buried Alive for 'Talking to Boys,'" *The Guardian,* February 4, 2010, www.guardian.co.uk/world/2010/feb/04/girl-buried-alive-turkey (accessed September 26, 2011).

42. "Chapter 3: Ending Violence Against Women and Girls," Honour Killings, United Nations Population Fund, State of World Population website, www .unfpa.org/swp/2000/english/ch03.html (accessed October 26, 2011).

43. Nicholas D. Kristof and Sheryl WuDunn, *Half the Sky: Turning Oppression into Opportunity for Women Worldwide* (New York: Knopf, 2009), 82.

44. Kiva is a nonprofit organization that aims to alleviate poverty by connecting

people worldwide through lending. They use the Internet and microfinancing to allow individuals to lend as little as US$25 to help others help themselves. Visit kiva.org for more information.

Part Six: Your Secret Weapon for Growing Up

1. Committee on Communications, "Children, Adolescents, and Advertising," *Pediatrics* 118, no. 6 (December 2006), www.communication.wsu.edu/mcmhp/pdf/AAP_statement.pdf (accessed October 24, 2011).
2. Maria Makino, Koji Tsuboi, and Lorraine Dennerstein, "Prevalence of Eating Disorders: A Comparison of Western and Non-Western Countries," *Medscape General Medicine* 6, no. 3 (2004): 49, www.ncbi.nlm.nih.gov/pmc/articles/PMC1435625 (accessed October 24, 2011).
3. Jay G. Silverman et al., "Dating Violence Against Adolescent Girls and Associated Substance Use, Unhealthy Weight Control, Sexual Risk Behavior, Pregnancy, and Suicidality," *Journal of the American Medical Association* 286, no. 5 (2001). See also "Teen Dating Violence Facts," available at www.clotheslineproject.org/teendatingviolencefacts.pdf (accessed October 13, 2011).
4. "Intimate Partner Violence in the U.S., Offender Statistics," Bureau of Justice Statistics, http://bjs.ojp.usdoj.gov/content/intimate/offender.cfm (accessed October 13, 2011).
5. Jessica Valenti, *The Purity Myth: How America's Obsession with Virginity Is Hurting Young Women* (Berkeley, California: Seal Press, 2009), 65.
6. Ibid., 66.

ACKNOWLEDGMENTS

There are so many people without whom this book would not exist.

First, I have to thank my parents, Cathy and Scott Zeilinger because without them I would not physically exist and therefore neither would this book. I would also not be the person I am today without them, and for that I will never be able to express enough gratitude.

Thanks to Brian Zeilinger for the title of this book, for being a never-ending source of brilliant ideas, and for always putting me in my place (in a completely feminist and appropriate kind of way).

Thanks to my grandparents, Miki and Bill Christgau, and the Berkowitz and Sabini families for your love and support.

A MILLION AND A HALF THANKS to Alison Schwartz, the most amazing agent in the entire world who plucked me from obscurity and then went above and beyond and even a little bit further than that working on this book. I admire you so much and will never be able to repay you for all that you have done for me.

Thanks to Brooke Warner for believing in this book and thanks to everybody at Seal Press who made it a reality.

Thanks to Courtney Martin, Jessica Valenti, Gloria Steinem, and all my feminist gurus who have supported me and believed in me from the start.

Thanks to the teachers who have inspired me over the years. Namely, thanks to Julia Griffin, my high school advisor and teacher, Brian Hart, who taught me Humanities in eighth grade, and Carrie Barnabei, who was never actually a teacher but was a constant source of support nonetheless. They helped set me on this journey, and I'll never forget that.

Thanks to the girls on the bench on the ramp (you know who you are) for loving me and supporting me and being the greatest friends anybody could ever hope for. Thanks to the guy from Strongsville for just being awesome. Thanks to my fellow strong, beautiful Barnard women.

Thanks to everyone who ever has or ever will read or contribute to The FBomb. You are the most inspiring, wonderful people and have taught me more than I could ever describe.

© ERIC MULL

ABOUT THE AUTHOR

Julie Zeilinger is originally from Pepper Pike, Ohio (for real), and is a member of the Barnard College Class of 2015. Julie is the founder and editor of The FBomb (www.thefbomb.org), a feminist blog and community for teens and young adults who care about their rights and want to be heard. Julie has been named one of the "Eight Most Influential Bloggers under 21" by *Women's Day*, one of the "New Feminists You Need to Know" by *More*, one of the "40 Bloggers Who Really Count" by *The Times* of London, and one of the "Most Interesting People of 2011" by *Cleveland Magazine*. Her writing has been published on The Huffington Post, Feminist .com, and *Skirt* magazine, among other publications. She hates people who talk two inches away from her face, loves brunch, and is fluent in sarcasm. Her website is at www.juliezeilinger.com.

Selected Titles from Seal Press

For more than thirty years, Seal Press has published groundbreaking books.
By women. For women.

F 'em!: Goo Goo, Gaga, and Some Thoughts on Balls, by Jennifer Baumgardner. $17.00, 978-1-58005-360-0. A collection of essays—plus interviews with well-known feminists—by *Manifesta* co-author Jennifer Baumgardner on everything from purity balls to Lady Gaga.

What You Really Really Want: The Smart Girl's Shame-Free Guide to Sex and Safety, by Jaclyn Friedman. $17.00, 978-1-58005-344-0. An educational and interactive guide that gives young women the tools they need to decipher the modern world's confusing, hypersexualized landscape and define their own sexual identity.

Get Opinionated: A Progressive's Guide to Finding Your Voice (and Taking A Little Action), by Amanda Marcotte. $15.95, 978-1-58005-302-0. Hilarious, bold, and very opinionated, this book helps young women get a handle on the issues they care about—and provides suggestions for the small steps they can take towards change.

Full Frontal Feminism: A Young Woman's Guide to Why Feminism Matters, by Jessica Valenti. $15.95, 978-1-58005-201-6. A sassy and in-your-face look at contemporary feminism for women of all ages.

Yes Means Yes: Visions of Female Sexual Power and A World Without Rape, by Jaclyn Friedman and Jessica Valenti. $16.95, 978-1-58005-257-3. This powerful and revolutionary anthology offers a paradigm shift from the "No Means No" model, challenging men and women to truly value female sexuality and ultimately end rape.

The Guy's Guide to Feminism, by Michael Kaufman & Michael Kimmel. $16.00, 978-1-58005-362-4. A hip and accessible guide that illustrates how understanding and supporting feminism can help men live richer, fuller, and happier lives.

Find Seal Press Online
www.SealPress.com
www.Facebook.com/SealPress
Twitter: @SealPress